2020 !

Poems for the
Working Class

By

Steven Berkoff

Grosvenor House
Publishing Limited

This book is published by
Grosvenor House Publishing Ltd
Link House
140 The Broadway, Tolworth, Surrey, KT6 7HT.
www.grosvenorhousepublishing.co.uk

This book is a work of fiction. Any resemblance to
people or events, past or present, is purely coincidental.

A CIP record for this book
is available from the British Library

ISBN 978-1-83975-130-1

CONTENTS

Songs

INTRODUCTION

These poems cover a great deal of time and are a reflection on the incidents and situations that occurred. Many were written during extensive touring with my theatre company and provided a much needed release between performances.

What a poem does is to somehow encapsulate very strongly ones feelings and responses to an event, which I feel could not be so dramatically put in prose.

There was only one way for me to write about the horrors of 9/11 and that was to put it into verse. *Requiem for Ground Zero* was an attempt to embrace the event in all its tragedy and to salute and memorialise the victims.

I wrote *Albion*, a cynical and somewhat satirical look at The Blair Years, I could think of no other way that this could be conveyed and lampooned, except in verse.

Uprising, which deals with one of the most horrific events that happened in Warsaw in the Second World War, has obsessed me for many years. The idea of a relatively small group of imprisoned Jews in the Warsaw Ghetto rising up against their Nazi torturers is one of the most inspiring and dramatic events of that war. It took place in 1943 and I have chosen to relate the events and be as true as possible to the facts, and to salute those incredible heroes who died bravely, rather than be shipped off to the German execution chambers.

Other poems that related to my touring of India were also inspired by the disgusting poverty I found and the brutal treatment of the underdog, or as they call them 'Dalits'.

S.B.

POEMS

ALBION

CHERIE:
Sod it and what a bloody fuss,
Just 'cause I claimed my rightful dues
Seven thousand five hundred bloody quid!
To keep my precious hair in place,
I mean I've got to look a PM's wife
And not a rotten beat-up slag
Just stepped out of EastEnders,
Or The Bill or other rotten bilge
The dumbed down population love,
So twice a day my man with magic fingers
Turns my ragged tresses into waves,
Of silky shimmering auburn coils,
That I might stand next to my man
My Tony, looking bright and proud,
Whilst we stretch out our spotless hands,
And gather precious Labour votes.
Like Bodicea I must seem,
The sunlight sparking little glints
Upon my new oiled precious curls,
That's worth a mere two fifty plus
A day, my darling don't you think?
Ach, how the filthy British Press
Can't wait to make their rancid stink!

TONY:
Can't be helped Cherie when you're on top,
The largest searchlight in the world
Is focused day and bloody night
On every move you do and what you say,
On every penny that you spend
On who you pass your bloody time with,

Who's your mates, how much you've got,
And has my hair changed back to black,
And am I fiddling from the State,
When we pissed off in a freebie jet,
To go to far off tropic climes,
Like we should wait on standby at Heathrow.
Yeah, just to show, we're noble, decent
Full of humble grace and good,
Oh! we should live like monks, all pure,
And wear a loincloth round our limbs,
We not exactly fiddlers or thieves,
I' ve made no fortune that's for sure,
Just some small perks of office, don't we all,
That's what they're there for, oil the state,
And grease a dirty palm or two,
But Cherie as I said, take care
We're in the stinking public eye,
A great big bloody, bulging orb, that sits above a filthy
    yelping mouth,
That just can't wait to squeal and shout,
So have a care, be subtle when you claim
Those dodge expenses, play the game!

CHERIE:
Oh come on Tone, you know I'm good,
And try to keep the fiddles low,
What ever I do, you're right, some bastard squeals,
They've got it in for me, and God knows why,
Cause if they can't quite get at you
As much as they would love to do,
Then coward like they attack your flank
And make out I'm some vile Medusa,
With a head of writhing snakes,
Or Lady Macbeth, Imelda Marcos,
And I hate the way the filthy Press
Must take my picture only when
My mouth is shaped just like a letterbox,

4

That's just so cruel, I can't help that
For that's what God gave me at birth.
But other times I'm quite pretty, I know,
But that's not what the Press do like to show.

TONY:
Oh come on Cherie, I know it's tough
But can't you comb your own hair, now and then,
I don't mean to be hard on you,
But millions of women seem able to,
And then there's less to pick on dear,
Much less cause to snipe and howl,
So be a little subtle in your tastes,
Your choice of mates, no let me rephrase that,
Under what bloody stone did you find that pair,
That tart, that gave you massages,
And dragged into our famous home,
That conman from Australia,
That lowdown oily thief you did befriend,
And even employ that bum to do a deal,
To buy some flaky property,
Now Cherie, where on earth's your head,
That you, a lawyer, could sink so low,
To entertain such low class trash,
Come on, wise up, that's why
The Press now leap on every move you make
And what's this with Australia,
That for a charity you palmed
Far more than they could raise themselves,
Now that does not go down too well,
Especially with our Ozzy friends,
Who send word back that you're a little,
Just a tad, demanding darling,
No let me rephrase that, a greedy bitch,
And that's what we must never be,
Or seem to be because we are New Labour!
Stand for fairness, honesty, not Tory greed,

For God's sake, you know better, you're not dumb, Cherie,
And what's these massive fees I hear you charge
For one hour's yakking in America,
Don't sink the ship, I had to tell you,
And since you brought it up,
About your bloody hair, I had to say,
Don't bring the heavens down on Blair!

CHERIE:
Oh, oh, oh, oh, oh!
Oh, that's very good, that's bloody good,
That you should preach to me about my friends
Just 'cause I found a rotten bloody apple
In a pile, that's human, that can happen,
Now and then
and tell me who's not been conned
Who not shafted, been cheated in their lives?
They're very bloody lucky or,
They're hermits living in a cave,
Half the bloody cabinets been ripped off,
Or exposed for stinking wealth and gain,
Or run to print and waving stinking knickers in the air,
Like that egg woman, what's her name,
Exposing our John Major, that sweet man,
For something private, between two souls,
A private shag that should be known
To only God and to themselves.
So intimate, so secret, and that cow,
Just like some dirty flasher in the park,
Bellows out her prize in print!
People have been killed for far, far less,
And being as blind as bloody bats,
Might make you extra sensory in other places,
For dear Dave Blunkett, sweet old soul,
Whom all the world admired and pitied,
Took his elbow when he crossed the road,
But he knew where to shove his stick,

He couldn't wait to dip his wick,
No, didn't need a helping hand,
But followed his nose, well, so to speak,
And there's plenty more, no doubt,
Who caused a blush on brave New Labours face,
And if I start with Tories, there's no end,
To sleaze, and slime and crookery,
Sex, scandal, robbery and con,
So Tony please, oh please,
Don't point your accusing finger,
Just at me, I'm really innocent,
It's just my hair the grubbies picked on, most unfair!
And what about that loony Ken,
Licking arse in China town
With far more relish than he downs
His chicken chop suey and his yen,
To stick giant eyesores every where
Huge phallus's to turn our city
Into some mini Manhattan-ugh
I think it's shitty!

LIVINGSTONE:
Ok, Red Ken they used to call me then,
They like to slap a handle on you,
Make it stick as if your life
Was just a single issue, just one cause,
Like you're sleeping with the Left,
When what we did, we changed the bloody
Face of London, gave it a town hall,
A grand majestic place, a heart,
A soul in London town,
But now, it's an aquarium,
Was once a gallery for the arts,
If you can call the sludge and muck
That now gets flung upon a wall,
In the name of art; no matter,
Every dog must have it's day.

And then they voted me for Mayor,
You gotta laugh, 'cause Tony cried,
They wanted some tired prat,
Some crony, mate, to put me out,
But, between just you and me,
you didn't have a bloody clue,
To what he was or stood for,
So Geoffrey Archer was the one,
Who had some balls, connections too,
But his old mate just stuck the knife in,
Shopped his friend, no doubt
For loot, cause them old Tories
Only move, when they can smell a bob or two,
Now that's a scumbag thing to do,
But then it suited me just fine.

REPORTER:
Were you afraid the scheme you had
Congestion charges might just fail?
The Labour party thought you mad;
And did that bother you at all?

KEN:
To tell you the truth the bolder the plan,
The greater chance to win the mob,
The masses can't be fooled, they know,
What's good for them, you know they do,
Congestion charges went like a bomb,
And we were first and now
The world will copy us, you'll see,
And think of all the millions
We'll have raised,
Of course to improve the roads
And make it safe for little ones.
And when I saw how well it worked,
I thought, hold on, those greedy autocrats,
Are so in love with their sweet cars,

They'll pay an extra three quid, yeah
And so we slapped it on and still they come,
And if you can't afford to pay,
Then get out of your stinking car
And take the bloody tube or bus,
It's cheaper and you'll get there fast.

REPORTER:
But what if you've got young kids,
Are old or handicapped,
What then? Or stuck in wheelchairs,
Have to carry heavy bags?

KEN:
We'll make concessions, course we will,
Apply and fill in countless forms
And then just slap a permit on your cars,
No, Were not just heartless beasts,
The underdog will be alright.

REPORTER:
But why does it cost so much to park,
Three quid or more an hour, then
If you are just a minute late
You'll find a great big yellow clamp,
And then you have to sit and wait,
And pay sometimes two hundred quid?
And do you think that's fair?

KEN:
I cannot say I like it, no I don't,
But then the clampers got to earn,
The meter man he's got to make,
A few bob extra for the state,
And then we've got to keep the streets
Quite safe and clear or else
The city's just a solid block,

Of stink and smoke and carbon choke,
So save the city, s'wot I say,
We'll control those clamping thieves
From getting too…industrious,
Yes, I know that they're a little keen.

REPORTER:
Industrious is just another word for theft,
I'd say when one disabled motorist,
Just paid three hundred quid to stop
Her precious motor being towed,
When it was plain for all to see,
Her disabled badge as clear as you and me.

KEN:
Oh yes, we'll put a stop to cowboys,
They're a pest that always feed upon the law
Don't worry mate, prison's too good,
For mugs like these, but like they're very rare.

REPORTER:
A motorbike was clamped outside
A petrol station while the owner asked
Directions from the staff inside;
His fine was two hundred and sixty five.

KEN:
As I said they're thieves galore out there,
It's in the British blood, we know,
Who doesn't fiddle nowadays is a saint.
Look at the scheming bastards
In the Commons, screwing thousands
For their 'second home', oh yeah,
And all legit of course, that's right,
But, and take my word, Red Ken
Will come down sodden hard with those,
Who use the law to make a buck.

REPORTER:
And what about the cameras everywhere,
That track, and capture every move
And fines are pouring through the doors
For just the slightest error
In your speed, a tiny blip,
A fraction over thirty, late at night,
With no one on the road,
And then you bleed for one day's wages,
Cross a line or do a turn,
And millions, millions pouring in
And do you think that's very fair?
Do you really think that's very fair?

KEN:
True we've got more cameras in our streets
Than any nation in the world,
So keep your nose clean my old son,
And stop your damned complaining whine,
You sound like some Gestapo guard,
So piss off to your filthy rag,
And use your arse to print the morning news.
I'm off to China now to do some good,
And show the way to run a city.
And anyway I'm mad for Chinese food.

TONY:
Look Cherie love, I've really got to bloody go,
Got some explaining that's for sure,
So let me get to my bench and do some spin,
They're waiting, drooling Tory scum,
To sink their bloody fangs in me,
And I'm the one, the head, the bloke
That has to take the bloody flak,
For some damned idiot's sodden joke!

11

CHERIE:
O shit, my darling, what's up now?
It seems that not a day can pass,
Without some wretched idiot fucking up,
And sticking his head right up his arse.
But what do you mean, 'a sodden joke'?

TONY:
This bloke, this idiot Charlie Clark,
Though not his fault, it's not his job,
To watch and guard the prison's gates,
He's only the Home Secretary,
And can't know all the rotten flaws
That make up our great nation state,
But one thousand and twenty three
Foreign criminals were released
Who should have been deported, can you believe!
And now these murderers, rapists, robbers too,
Like some foul poison in our blood,
Contaminates our wholesome British state.
Oh shit and piss and bollox too...
Is this a Labour party that we have, or zoo?

CHERIE:
At least he's not caught shagging, that's a plus.
These days it seems to me, cause men
Can't keep their flies done up, without
Some paper paying off a squealer,
So that's a small mercy, I should say.

TONY SHRUGS AND EXITS.

REPORTER:
10,265 foreign prisoners in England and Wales in
    February 2006.
Total population: 76,760.
The highest per capita in Europe.

Wormwood scrubs hold the highest number of foreign
prisoners; from 85 countries speaking 24 languages.
The B.N.P [expects to] increases its vote substantially.

JOHN PRESOTT.
Okay, okay, I had a shag,
Big sodden deal, yeah, forget the IRA,
Forget the melting icecaps, global warming,
Osama Bin liner and the rest,
A few bombs in a seaside town,
And bodies shattered, missing limbs,
Forget all that, that's nothing much;
Ok Iran will get the bomb,
And Bush is getting very horny,
Whenever his finger's near the button,
That will send us all to kingdom come,
He gets that kind of randy look,
But that's okay, we'll handle that,
More hurricanes, and major storms,
That sea is rising every day,
We must stop burning fossil fuel,
But tell that to the big boys
Running Shell and Exon and the rest,
Tell them, they'll stick two fingers in your face.
BUT if I had a little shag,
a little frolic, I get front page,
Front 'effing page, like this is life,
The world will crumble,
And mighty states will fall,
And global warming will shoot up,
"Cause two Jag Prescott"
Dipped his wick, oh hell,
Bring back the guillotine!
For bloody Jesus' sake, get real,
So sorry Tony I fucked you up,
I know you got a plateful now,
And every slimey Tory dog,

Will wag their rotten tails in glee,
But we'll get over this no fear,
Tomorrow is another day,
I mean, it's not a crime alright,
And I have been married forty years
Or forty-five to be exact.
Joe Public ain't no mugs they know,
A bloke ain't normal without some snatch,
It's human, natural to want a squeeze,
Come on the work is hard, you need to feel,
A piece of crumpet now and then,
And can't just bung it in the same old hole.
Of course I love my missus, course
But every man gets tempted, don't you know?

TONY:
But there's a famous saying, yes?
Upon your own doorstep do not shit,
So what you did was taking risks,
To jeopardize your future life,
To bonk the bird who works for you
So everyone around you knows,
Illicit liaisons have a smell
And those around you take a whiff,
And soon sniff out that something is amiss.
And then the boyfriend quickly twigs
And runs into the gaping jaws,
of our salivating prying Press,
Who could not possibly ask for more.
So how's the missus, Pauline, cope?

JOHN:
Oh she's alright, she's great, she understood,
She knows I've been a great big dope,
Of course we issued a statement, sure,
That said she's devastated by it all,
For twenty grand I was sold out,

Can't blame the bloke cause that's the way,
A slag can earn a living nowadays,
But then again it's cooled the heat,
On Charlie Clarke's small escapade,
I mean a thousand villains on our streets
Is not a nice thing now to contemplate,
I mean what I did wouldn't hurt a fly,

TONY:
Oh come on John, the public eye,
Want leaders they look up to, love,
Admire, respect, and doff their cap,
A little more than human and that's hard,
To set an example, be a saint,
At least that's what we try to do, alright,
The image that we must create,
A sense of decency and probity,
A man of honour without chinks,
Let me rephrase that bit, I mean,
It's a tough role you have to play,
To be Statesman, a little grey
Perhaps but that's ok, but don't,
Don't ever show you're like the mob,
Don't be a man of needs and weakness for a tart,
They don't want you to be like them,
Scurvy, greedy on the bloody make,
Fiddle your expenses, dodge the tax,
A secret number in your mobile phone,
And dirty rendezvous with dodgy birds.
So bloody be a Statesman John,
That's what we all expect from you,
So be a champ and not a chump.

JOHN:
It's funny yeah, how all good guys,
Upright and moral, spouting Christ,
Their mouths are always full of God,

Their fingers never in other pies,
Are the biggest murderers in the world,
Gung ho for war and nuclear strike,
And freedom to bear arms so kids kill kids,
And fuck the Kyoto Treaty, cost too much,
And never think and never feel,
That this great world is running out,
Is running out of water, good clean air,
Is running out of our great beasts,
That roamed so free in jungles wild,
Is running out of good clean fish,
Not poisoned by mercury, industrial filth,
Where are the laws to curb those brutes,
The laws Bill Clinton strove to make,
Before his cock became his noose,
To hang him high and jeer and spit,
Now, your pal Bush, forgive me Tone,
I'm sure his zip's done up, no doubt,
Just like his hardened devil's heart,
He spouts "God bless you" every day,
"We'll win this goddam war!" Oh sure,
It maybe just a paradox,
But I'd rather trust a man, who loves his cock!

CHERIE: (running in)
Oh did I hear the sound of cock?
Oh John it's you, are you ok?
Been so worried 'bout you today,
But please don't fret it soon will pass,
And Tony knows it all too well,
The stink of scandal doesn't last.

JOHN: (dour)
Oh really, didn't know that love,
Poor John Profumo bit the dust,
And to the very end, poor sod,
The Press spoke only of his days of lust.

16

CHERIE:
But that was then and with a whore,
Some scheming low class piece of trash,
But your bit's quite a sweetie pie,
Looks quite chunky, lovely arse,
And she's called Tracy, so it's **Working Class!**
You've not betrayed the Labour ranks
Like poor old David Blunkett, no,
The silly old devil couldn't see,
The baseness of his treachery,
To stick it in a Tory bitch,
I mean, that really is the pits!
Al least dear John, you dropped your pants,
Within our local Labourhood,
And then the stink's a touch less blue
Than pink.

TONY:
Ok, and that's settled now,
No question that I keep you on,
You're far too valuable to lose,
Just over a bloody bit of flooze,
So bear in mind just what I said,
It's better dead I think, Dear John
Than to be caught pants down in bed.

TONY EXITS.

CHERIE:
Mustn't be late for the Queen's party!

VOX POPULI:

DAILY MAIL. (Stephen Glover)   SCREEN
"These two men (Prescott and Clarke) have succeeded in
    turning this fag end of an administration into a farcical
    Carry On film. It might be called Carry On Regardless.

However grave are the charges of incompetence against Clarke and impropriety against Prescott both men are determined to cling to power. Prescott in particular has much to lose, not only the ministerial jag but two grace and favour residences and all the perks that come with them…if the incompetent Charles Clarke and the sleazy John Prescott are the twin symbols of Tony Blair's dying administration there is no doubt in my mind as to which of them is worst."

VOX POPULI:
It's hard, to run the N.H.S
But bloody hell we pay our dues,
For forty sodden tax drained years,
I paid each week my insurance stamp,
But now I'm getting old and worn,
And see my local doctor chap
He says, a specialist is what I need
Cause I'm having some trouble when I pee,
Now it could be prostate cancer, yeah,
Or it could be something benign,
But sod me there's a waiting list,
A mile sodden long, you have to wait,
And in the meantime sit and fret,
Or fret and shit yourself with fear,
And so I wait and wait and then,
I get a note, they'll see me now,
So in I went, "Lay down," he says,
"And keep your knees up to your chest."
And then he sticks his finger up my arse.
"You got a fucking lump," he said,
"We'll do a scan a check it out,
You got a big enlargement there,
But we can trim it for you,
Take it out, cause if you don't,
It really might get really bad."
"Okay," I says, "Do watcha can,

Cause I can't piss no more like a man."
"Of course you might not fuck again,
You'd lose your hard-on for a while,
And sometime you will piss your pants,
And you'll be sterile for all time,
But that's a tiny price I'd say,
If you can live another day."
"Okay, sod me I've had my day,
'Spose it's the price I have to bloody pay,
Don't want the cancer spreading to my joints."
"Cause that's a risk you'll have to take."
So then I said,
"Yeah take it out, if that's the best."
And then they all replied "Oh yes,
But we can't do it for a while,
You'll have to wait a bit my friend,
Cause all the world's checking their ends,
So much chatter 'bout it now,
That blokes are pouring in, so now,
Just wait a bit, we'll let you know."
And so I did, the months flew past,
And still no word and now my arse,
Has got a pain you can't believe,
I'm getting bloody headaches too,
So I went back to have a check,
I mean it's great, it really is,
Like when it really works that is,
They did a scan and then they dropped,
A bloody bomb upon my head,
"I'm sorry mate," they said, "But you've
Metastasised." Cor, fuck, what's that?
"It's spread, the bloody cancer's spread,
It's not the end though of the world,
It's bound to happen now and then,
You should have seen us earlier."
"But I did!" I squealed, "You had no time."
"Er yes, but earlier than that I think,

No matter, a dose of chemo will set you right,
That'll help control the rot,
You'll lose your horn and might go bald,
But that's a tiny price to pay
If you can live another day.
Just wait a bit, we'll let you know."
And so I did, it's quicker now,
I got my letter, "Come in," they said,
They shoved this chemo in my veins,
Cor did I feel like bloody shit,
But after, it's better and less pain.
I had my check-up in six months time,
"I'm sorry mate, to have to say,
Your liver's gone to bloody pot."
A transplant? "No, bit old for that,
But we can give you another splat,
Of chemo, radiation too!
But that's a tiny price to pay.
If you can live another day."
So I went home and told the wife,
She wrapped me up all nice and warm,
"Don't you worry mate," she said,
As she tucked me into my bed,
And so we wait, the weeks flew past,
And then I thought, oh fuck it, yes,
I've had enough chemo, give it a miss,
So now they give me morphine now,
To ease the pain, it feels quite nice,
I've got a few months left, I think,
"You should have seen us earlier on."
"I did," I said, "You made me wait,
You made me bloody wait, ok!"
"Er, yes, but earlier than that,
And we might have caught it just in time!"
I know, yer doing your best for me,
Our health service's unique, it's fine
If you can get treated in fucking time!
Yeah... if you get treated in fucking time..!

HEALTH SECRETARY PATRICIA HEWITT:
Oh you can't imagine the horrendous roar,
Two thousand angry nurses shriek,
It turned into a bloody farce,
Who says that women never think,
Are just blobs of emotion, pain,
And cannot reason, understand,
Get an overview, discuss,
There is a bitter truth in that,
As health secretary, it's my job,
To set the guidelines, mark the course,
Tell the bloody nurses how,
We've made our health service a golden cow,
That's worshipped, idolised around the world,
I know there've been redundancies,
I know that hurts, it hurts me too,
I know the cutbacks, layoffs pinch
A bit and make us wince,
We've got a billion plus deficit
And that's enough to sink a ship,
So naturally we've got to cut and slash,
So be a trifle understanding,
I know the doctors, some of them,
Take home two hundred and fifty thousand pounds!
That's just another bloody error,
Another cock-up, we'll get it fixed,
Of course we will, like everything
Will be alright, trust me, yes?
But this year was the very best,
Ok! We're really making strides,
And I don't think it will be more,
Than seven thousand nurses maybe ten,
Will be redundant, though it could be less,
We'll sort it out, please don't be sore,
Don't act like headless chickens, silly birds,
Think of the pay rises you have had,

Now don't be angry, hear me out,
Our waiting times reduced, lives saved, (boos)
Oh bollax, I've just had enough!
And since it seems you've had enough
I'll make my exit, sod you all.
One day the Tories will be there
And then you'll see, my angry girls,
The National Health Service in complete despair!

(Boo!, Boo!, Jeers, Get Off!, Shut Up!, Poser!, Fake!)

TONY:
Oh shit and piss and bollox too,
Poor Johny Prescott's on the blink,
The bitch has gone and spilled her guts!
And for a wadge off filthy dosh,
Has sold her other hole,
Her mouth, as low class whores are wont to do,
So he was caught between two slags,
Her boyfriend shot his bolt for twenty grand,
And now his cow has gone to press.
Oh why do women behave like this?
That for a pound will sell their flesh,
Humiliate a man who was their friend,
For two years was his bit of fluff,
His life and soul, his joy and spice,
Not just a whore picked from off the street,
Who runs to the gutter press and squeaks,
That is her trade, is all she's got,
A grimy box both north and south.
But here's a woman, was his friend,
And to be shafted at both ends,
First her slimy bloke tells all
And then she jumps in on the act,
I mean that villainous, bloody hell,
And John's just like a poor old bull,
Being stabbed on every slide,

22

Bewildered and damned crucified,
By every villain that wants a piece
Of his damned flesh on which to feast.
His 'misconducts' a private affair,
But now all knives for him are out.

CHERIE;
Hey Tone, don't whine and bloody spout!
Just thank God you've not been caught
With your trousers at half mast,
That's 'cause you've a pretty wife,
Who you still fancy, am I right?
Just why on earth can't men, excuse the word,
I'd rather call them pimps okay,
The ones that act like backstreet thugs,
who make their money out of whores,
Just how on earth do we allow
This scurvy bunch of dogs,
To milk these scabby tarts and make their dough,
An 'agent' who doth specialise
In fuck and bloody tell the Press,
And sure you jail a dirty pimp,
Who earned his money out of whores,
A dirty pimp who feeds upon a woman's flesh,
And yet these tarts perform a service,
Some will say are necessary and help blokes
Frustrated or without a hole,
To stick their lonely dicks into.
And yet these other 'whores' perform no service
But to soil and wound their client,
Humiliate, defile and taint,
Whilst their agent gets well paid,
Who quickly flogs it in the Press,
For what? For 'public interest' so they claim,
And not for a dumbed down public's taste,
To sneer and laugh, cackle and spit,
Help to destroy a human life,

His family, children and all he's got,
His pride, his worth, his years of strife
Awards and honours smashed to dust,
His friends cool off and draw away,
Colleagues will shun his society,
And all for bloody what, Christ's sake!
Because some dirty slut decides,
To give herself one great payday!
If you can jail a rotten pimp,
Then make a law that sends to jail,
All those that earn their money out of whores!!

TONY:
Oh Cherie dear, I wish I could,
But the great freedom of our land,
Allows some scum, sadly, to get the upper-hand,
But free speech must prevail when sweet or sour,
The press is free and must be so,
We have some filters up to catch
Some racist trash and prejudice,
Egregious rot that sure contaminates,
The fairplay we are famous for,
And now that hook-hand beast's behind steel bars,
For preaching hate and death in our good land,
While in their own detested home
The heads are swiftly severed from their necks,
Oh sure we let them preach their filth too long,
Impressing those too innocent and young,
And now we've shut that particular door,
But I'm afraid we can't do more,
Or else we'll be a very different state,
If more doors are shut tight I fear,
We may resemble those nations we hate.
[Clarke enters puffing]
Ok, Charles, what's your news?
Please shed a little sunshine on this mess,
Just something positive, I long to hear,

Of shit, I can't take too much more,
Your thousand criminals that you let loose,
To wander round and kill and rape,
Perhaps you'll tell me, you gave them the boot!

CLARKE:
One ray of sunshine that's for sure,
Your Johnny Prescott's shoved my tale,
Right off the front page, so that's okay,
His mangy tart spilling her guts,
Has drawn the Nation's Press like salivating mutts,
Who love nothing so much as sniff at crutch,
To leap and whelp at sordid tales,
Of knickers, oral sex, the lot,
The readers love this more, far more,
Than murderers on the loose and increased tax,
A few more dozen killings in Iraq,
A thousand dead, Afghanistan
Oil that's reaching record costs,
All this means nothing when you read,
That Prescott's hand slides up her skirt,
And bunk-ups on the office desk.
So to the point we've got some time,
I'm on the case believe me Tone,
It really looks much worse than it really is,
We know the Press are on us like a dose of clap,
Cause out of that one thousand slags,
That dirty foreign muck that you let in.
I wasn't there then so don't blame me,
There's only 79 real scum,
Real killers, drug lords, rapist dogs.
And we'll catch them Tone, no fear,
And ship them out to kingdom come,
Even though they beg and squeal (asylum),
"Oh asylum please, they'll chop us up,
If we go home." We know that con,
It a familiar song, so Tone,

We're on the case, so please don't sweat,
But heads will roll when we find out,
What silly ponces shine their pants,
In our great government offices and step on
Them like bloody ants!

TRACY:
I had to go public cause I felt abandoned,
I felt he let me down, and hung out to dry,
No, I didn't do it just for the dosh,
Although £250,000 will come in handy, sure,
But that doesn't make me into a bloody whore,
Corse not, I'm really just so sweet,
He came onto me, just like I was a piece of meat,
No, I didn't do it for the cash,
Oh no, I did it to clear my name,
Like I didn't go home and think,
Oh my God I'm fucking the D.P.M
It's a lot of dosh, I know, quids in,
But I didn't do it for the cash,
I enjoyed his attention, felt cared for,
But that doesn't make me into a bloody whore,
He carried me into his bedroom then,
He started kissing and undressing me,
We did it then and it was nice,
And then one day we both got hot,
And it was then I sucked his cock,
And after he got bacon butties for us all,
But I did so like the service for the dead,
He took me to on that grey morn,
For the boys in Iraq at the great St Paul's,
But then he seemed to get the horn,
Since after he just rushed me to his flat
Because he wanted sex again!
But no, I felt I had to clear my name.
But I didn't do it for the cash,
The actual figure I left to Max;

Max Clifford who takes care of girls like me.
£250,000 that's not a bad score
But that doesn't turn me into a whore,
Does it? Had to speak out and set the record straight,
That's what my mum said and she's right,
And I don't think I've ruined his life,
He should have thought before he slid his hand
Between my legs 'cause he might find
Something that one day just might bite.
But I didn't do it for the cash, oh no,
It just eases the pain a bit,
£250,000 will I have to pay tax?
A good accountant should take care of that!

NICK GRIFFIN: (B.N.P)
The British National Party is your hope,
I mean I can't deny it's been a bonus,
Can't deny that bunch of dopes,
In power to whom you gave your votes,
That bunch of bums, have shown you what they are,
We couldn't ask for more, my god,
You couldn't invent it, what a soap,
The people are beginning to wise up
And then you'll see an avalanche for the B.N.P.
We've had enough and were not racist,
No, just want to keep what's England, right?
Nothing wrong with that my friends,
We had our few odd whackos in the past,
But they've been sorted, ironed out the chinks.
Voluntary resettlement not bloody force,
We'll help those to return to their own lands,
That's fair and just and then we'll help
Those poorer with a lump of cash,
But no one will be forced that's not our way,
A little persuasion maybe but that's all
They've been a cause for rising crime,
And also Britain's cultural decline,

And let's be fair to us, for God's sake,
Stop non-European immigration,
It mucks the very fabric up
Of our society, pollutes the line,
Of Englishness which is our Nation's bloody spine.
Unless you want more bombs on buses and on tubes,
More violence in the streets,
And drug gangs rife in every town,
And wait more years to get a home
While others just off bloody boats,
Get right to the head of the sodden line,
Wait months to get a cancer test,
Watch your kids fall down the hole,
Of unemployment 'cause at school
They were, held back,
'Cause few could speak the English tongue.
D'ya want that? Then you know to whom
Your precious vote should really go,
To that bunch of tossers with their pants,
Around their knees,
With a leader who'll do anything to please
His master, lick his hand,
Condemn to death a few more brave and noble men,
From Briton for that stinking pit of filth,
That bottomless swamp,the Middle East
We've been too soft on paedophiles,
That's why, my friends, no sooner out,
They prey the streets again, so all I say,
Is hanging just too good for them?
But rather we'll bring back the rope,
Then see another woman or child defiled.
You want to rid the streets of yobs, the trash,
The drunken swill that stains our towns?
Then bring back National Service, that's the way
To train our sullen youth and make then fit,
And don't give me all that Hitler tripe,
We're past all that, all parties

When they start, attract some rotten apples,
Some frustrated scum but we are clean,
And even British Jews can join the party.
Of course we've had some problems with them in the past,
The Jews I mean, I know I've made
Some accusations, claimed, that they control
The Press and brainwash us with liberal shit,
Cause worldwide violence 'cause of Israel,
But now we've got it sorted, they're not half bad,
And some will stand as councillors for us,
And so you see, we've got a better policy.
Ok, you've got the point I think,
You don't want religious fanatics in our street,
Preaching hate against our race,
When they're our bloody guests, stealing the dole,
Taking the bread from out your mouth,
Bleeding the health service, making you wait.
You want your England back do you?
Just vote for us and then you'll see
What we can do. Vote, B.N.P!

G.W.BUSH: (on video-link phone)
Hey Tony, how are you, kid, okay?
You know Tony your influence is good,
The way you speak, concise and clear,
And don't think it's gone in one ear,
And out the other,
No way dear pal, I took a tip,
And now I no longer sound like shit,
Or like a plank of wood, oh no.
I used to watch you enviously old pal,
Your words just pouring out so flawlessly,
Whilst I just stumbled like a drunken bum,
But boy I watched you, took the hint,
Improved my act and now can talk
Without a script, sometimes, that is.
It's practice right, so Tony how's your game?

What's that, Iraq? Oh not again,
Forgive me Tone, I've had it up to here,
With all those weeping liberals gushing forth,
So took the weekend for a game of golf,
And boy it really clears your head,
And you should get out more and hit some strokes,
It puts things in perspective pal.
I know you've had some flack out there,
With Prescott's shags and Cherie's hair.
It's never easy being the chief,
But it's a great high don't you think?
Iraq's okay and since you ask,
Our boys are doing fine, just fine.
I know they whine 4000 dead,
Like you can stage a war that don't cost a cent,
You can't make omelettes without cracking eggs,
And we are bringing democracy, my friend!
We bought that to Nazi Germany,
To Japan who never knew of such a thing,
And did it cost, of course it did,
But was it worth it, you tell me,
So whats a few thousand kids, it's sad, we know,
But listen, more are killed on roads,
But you don't say close down the roads,
That is the price you pay for freedom.
So everyone has got a voice,
Not just a few weird psychos, hatching plots
And crazy loonies building nuclear bombs,
Who talk of wiping out whole states.
We put those maniacs in a home out here,
The Madhouse, till they vegetate.
But out there they're turned into kings,
Who rule like ancient tyrants, kill,
All who disagree with their foul ways,
So Tony, give my love to Cherie,
And pop on over when you can,
Love you to join us for a game,

Of blasting nuclear sights in old Iran!
Yo Blair!

TONY: (smiling)
He's not so bad as the Press make out,
He's got a few good points, he has,
They all just see him with one eye,
That's jaundiced, out of synch, malign,
We know he's not the brightest guy alive,
It doesn't take a genius to see he's...
Let me rephrase that, just a simple guy,
But basically good hearted, old fashioned maybe,
Believes he's with the good guys 'gainst the bad,
But he can be persuaded to believe,
That global warming's not a fantasy,
It just takes him a little time,
He shouldn't have changed those laws that Clinton made,
To protect environment, beast and man,
But then he's just badly advised,
Allows too much the business beasts to have their say,
Global corporation, oil and steel,
Polluters of the air and seas,
But, think, these are the last years he will reign,
And then his time over,
What relief.
But I'm still here, I have to be,
I really must take special care,
Of our most wonderful destiny!

VOX or CHORUS

EVENING STANDARD, APRIL 24th
"Oh yes, we're getting richer everyday
So Labour, New that is,
Is helping us,
The rich to get even richer, and that's good,
We don't have to wear clog shoes,

And sit in smelly pubs quaffing warm beer,
And talk of miners' strikes and live
On council estates, with piss stained lifts,
Not seen a cloth cap in some years,
Or hob-nailed boots, a choker round your throat,
That old allegiance to the Working Class,
With greasy spoon caffs, heart numbing tripe,
Eggs and bacon swimming in fat,
Fat beer bellies and heart attacks,
Dumbed down workers ready to strike,
For any little infringement on their rights.
Remember that ponce who took weeks off,
Because he had an injury, he said,
And made the railways for whom he worked,
Pay his wages while the bastard shirked,
Then he was caught out playing squash,
"It helps my leg to heal," he whined,
And then, quite right, he got the sack
And damn it if he didn't call a strike!
I s'pose you get a bad egg now and then,
The rot that gets inside the system, brings it down,
But now the workers eat in bistro pubs, no less,
Not stinking boozer, a rollup in their brown stained
     fingers,
They own a second-hand Mercedes,
A giant flat-screen TV in the house,
The kids tickling computer keys,
The missus has a second car,
A fistful of credit cards in her purse,
And fly to Thailand for a Xmas break,
They'll fix your plumbing, no sweat mate!
50 quid an hour is all it takes.
Now everybody's rich or on the scam,
Since this is New Labour, get rich quick,
That is unless you're a teacher or a nurse,
And anyway they work for love not wealth,
And thank the Gods for that I say,

Or we'd be well and truly lumbered.
And yet, you must admit, some wealth is good,
And you should be able to buy just what you want,
It spreads the wealth around it does.
And if you want a peerage or a gong,
And you can pay a bob or two,
What's really wrong with that, come on?
You help the state old chap and it helps you,
And then the really wealthy produce wealth,
For all the others in the chain,
So why should they pay all that tax?
So, off-shore havens are a must,
Not for you, you Working Class,
You're on the fiddle as it is,
(Nurses and teachers I exempt).
We need our billionaires, of course we do,
They hold the nation fast together, they are the glue
Their wives live in tax shelters, but so what?
They'll always drop a few bob in the pot.
Like that fat geezer, terrific bloke
His missus lives in Monte Carlo,
And who sends a billion million now and then,
To help the old girl out,
He didn't pay one penny's worth of tax on that.
And you might say, you whiners, whingers and sour
    grapes,
The money might have saved some lives,
Shortened a waiting list or two,
Built a school, improved facilities,
But look at all the good these big boys do at home,
With cut-price supermarkets selling trash,
And all the thousands they employ.
So don't begrudge their little scams,
New Labour mate, it's there for you.
And it's damned good, just look around,
Canary Wharf, the Dome, the Eye,
It's become a tourist paradise,

You got a Tesco on every high street,
Selling the swill you love to eat,
To make you fat as pigs and stink,
But think! You're free! Do what you like.
New Labour's made us great I think!
CHERIE: (comes in with hair on end)
Oh Tony, look, I'm doing it myself,
You see, I'm combing my own hair,
It's really quite exciting so don't fret,
Those bastards in the Press will shut up now,
And snipe and spit at someone else,
Oh Tony, you'll be just so proud,
So what's the matter sweetheart, you look sad,
What's up my pet, that makes you frown?

TONY:
Cherie, the entire town of London's turned quite blue,
We've lost the bloody nation more or less,
Those bloody Tories have swept in,
And swallowed up whole chunks of England,
And thrown us into the garbage bin;
Hammersmith, Fulham and Camden too,
That we have ruled for 30 years,
Is now a stinking Tory seat.
Oh hell, oh spite, that we should be so thrashed,
So whipped by this cycle riding Cameron sprite,
But never mind my dear, we're not beaten yet,
We're still in power in the seat,
And sitting in Great Downing Street,
And that will be for some years to come, I think.

CHERIE:
Do you think it was that awful stink,
When Prescott's arse was wobbling in the air,
And his tart Tracy screaming everywhere?
Or Clarke asleep while rapists and murderers walked the
    streets?
Or that bitch Hewitt in the NHS,

Telling nurses how great we are,
While sacking them in thousands; that does jar.
Or is the fiddles from MPs,
Falsely claiming stacks of quids,
For second homes they rarely see,
Or is it the price of everything shooting up,
While millionaires are richer than before,
While supermarket owners pay no tax,
And keep their dosh abroad, could it be that?
And giant new Tescos open every week,
And drive away the small nice shops,
From every town and village street,
Until each town will look the same,
With horrid super malls and parking lots.
Or could it be those parking laws,
That spy on every tiny flaw,
And fine car owners huge amounts,
With trivial offences, parking
Just a minute more than they should do,
Or is it the congestion charge that hurts
The poor while the rich just howl
With glee to have the streets a little free,
For their gigantic SUVs?
Or is it just the crime waves growing,
Getting larger everyday,
While guns now spreading like the plague,
Or is it the inheritance tax that bites chunks
From a life time's savings, that's been taxed
Already, could be that,
Or maybe, darling, it's the war,
Which daily claims the lives and limbs
Of British soldiers, brave young men,
Who went there under false pretences,
At least that's what they think,
Of course they're wrong, we kicked that scum,
That Saddam bastard out,
But is it really any better now,

Or maybe they just want a change,
I think that's it, what do you think?
Or could it really be my hair?
I often wonder and it drives me to despair!

TONY:
Well Cherie, now you ask, I have to say,
It didn't help, it didn't help
To show that nation that we spent that dosh,
£8000 or nearly that,
That's what the people focus on,
I know it's bloody trite to think,
While murderers stalk our British streets,
And bloody bombers blow us up,
And oil is getting dearer every day,
And in the end your bloody follicles,
Could make a dent in Labour's walls.
And then, my God, the Tories will come pouring,
The dam is broke and all junk values,
Tory sleeze and sell the bloody lot,
The NHS will go to hell,
And then the awful green wellies shriek,
'Cause they can't hunt their bloody beasts,
And so my dear even your lovely hair,
Which if one day you will learn to comb,
Will help reduce my sad despair.

CHERIE:
Look Tone, I think you're going round the twist,
It's not my bloody barnet only mate,
You read the papers, what do they say?
That MPs are on the fiddle, creaming dosh,
Rich sods like Barbara Follet claim their thousands,
Whose husband Ken is worth £14 million,
Got a country house that's worth
Another two million more or less,
Plus for one and a half million more,

A lovely holiday pad in Antigua,
A home in Cape Town and a flat in Soho,
And yet she claims £76,357 quid,
For four years, oh that's very smart.
Oh, it's for the cleaning bills and food,
Oh sure, and they're all up to it,
And what do you suppose your voters think,
That MPs are a pack of fiddling crooks,
So get your hounds out, route them out,
Give them a thrashing and you'll see,
The 'people' might then just believe,
New Labour sticks to principals, OK!?

CHORUS: [Extract from Richard 2]
This blessed plot, this earth, this realm, this England,
This nurse, this teaming womb of royal kings,
Feared by their breed and famous by their birth,
This land of such dear souls
This dear, dear land,
Dear for her reputation through the world,
IS now leased out, I die pronouncing it,
Like to a tenement or poultry farm,
England bound in the triumphant sea,
Whose rocky shore beats back the envious seige,
Of watery Neptune is now bound in with shame,
With inky blots and rotten parchment bonds,
That England that was wont to conquer others
Hath made a shameful conquest of itself...

TONY:
People forget, just how it was,
And do you want those days again,
When all your wealth, your assets too,
Were sold off to the highest bidder,
Your trains, your services that you cherish,
Your post that never comes each day on time,
A health service in ruins, doctors fleeing,

To the highest bidder,
And do you want those times again,
Schools jam packed and teachers underpaid,
A phone service that's torn apart,
And fortunes being squeezed from you each day,
That is the legacy that you inherited,
Siding up to villains in the world,
And giving sustenance to murderers and torturers,
Like Pinochet and other gangsters,
And do you want those times again?
Or stand by idle while thousands are wiped out,
In Kosovo; but we went in, in '99
Oh yes we did, and thank God that we did,
And put those murderers to flight.
Or do you want those times again when we stand
By and watch, unless it's for our own gain.
And do you want those times again?...

CHERIE.
Oh shit and piss and flaming arseholes too!
They've done it once again, the balloons gone up,
Oh why, just once, they cannot keep their cool,
I'm talking darling about the bloody Jews!

BLAIR.
Oh dear, now what have they done now?
You mean the TAX dodging Sir Phillip Green

CHERIE.
No not him!

BLAIR.
Or Michael Grade has come unstuck ..?

CHERIE.
Not him.

BLAIR.
Or Michael Winner wants his flaming knighthood..

CHERIE.
No no, not him!

BLAIR.
Has Harold Pinter spat on me yet again?

CHERIE.
Oh yes.. but no.. not him .. not him!

BLAIR.
That Shirley Porter woman's back, the one who bribed for
    votes..?

CHERIE.
Yes, she's back but no not her!

BLAIR.
Killing Christian babies, drinking blood,
Or are they simply poisoning wells?

CHERIE.
Ah now you're getting closer Tone..
The Jews are bombing Lebanon to bits!
To bits and little pieces and for what?
For just a little killing of their soldiers,
Israeli ones and kidnapping the rest,
So now inflamed, inspired for revenge,
They're blasting all and sundry, in their fury.
For heavens sake Tone, the I.R.A. Near blew
Old Thatcher and her cabinet to Kingdom come,
And did we turn a bloody hair,
Or did we blast Dublin to bits?
Oh did we hell! We just turned round
And said, piss off, we'll make a deal

39

And so you did Tone releasing all those killers,
To buy a little peace and quiet,
So you should go and sort it out,
Just like you did the IRA,
And you're so good at that ..they'll listen to you Tone.

BLAIR.
Look, the Middle East's a never healing sore,
A filthy cess pit that's sucks you down,
And all the lunatics in the world are there,
It's not that I don't like the Jews, I do,
In fact, we use them all the time,
Except when like Lord Levy they start
Flogging peerages, I mean that does get up the nose,
Of those muck rakers in the press.
It's in the blood, they can't help it,
Like when their granddads flogged old rags,
From ancient carts in Petticoat Lane,
But now I'm just a little tired dear
It's been a heavy couple of months
And now I think it's time to pack,
Our swimsuits, sun block and some shorts
And take off to some balmy clime

SECRETARY RUSHES IN

SECRETARY:
Oh dear P.M.. the news is bleak,
In some way... not in others, I think.
The good news is we exposed a plot,
To blow our planes to Kingdom come.
Thank god I say our agents sharp
Antennae, now on full alert,
To register the slightest twitch,
The merest sneering greasy glint,
From those who wish to do us harm
With poison in their evil hearts,
And endless cruelty in their souls..

40

BLAIR.
So what the good news?

SEC.
That was it, yes that's it, that we exposed,
That filthy sullen crew of wretched scum,
Who, brought up to respect our trust,
Were educated by our schools,
Their parents drawing weekly dole, meanwhile,
Free treatment at the hospitals,
And grabbing first class council flats,
By virtue of their seething broods,
And yet in spite of this, in spite of all,
That we have done for them, they then,
Decide to reward us by
Murder, mayhem, horrors untold,
But thank God we snared the fiends
Saving us from slaughter unimaginable!

CHERIE.
Oh Tone, one woe follows another heels,
And then the fiends, those drippy libbs
And feminist freaks all point at you!

BLAIR.
At me you say?

CHERIE.
Of course, you know how they love to blame,
The countries saviour, point their greasy finger,
Accuse you of cowtowing to the USA,
For so quickly joining Bushes posse,
Whom half the world has cast as Satan,
And now you're cast as Satan's emissary,
Ready to obey his every whim,
So think! What's best to do, my prince,
Eradicate this stain the nation thinks,

That you have cast upon the land,
Rid the country of the plague,
This violence that creeps from every door,
That seeps like puss from every wound,
Oh Tone, we are no longer safe,
No plane, no train, no boat, no bus,
Can we feel safe, secure, as once we did,
When just to be in England was a haven,
Home and sanctuary, a shelter..
For those who fled from hostile shores,
Where torture, execution and rape,
Imprisonment for uttering simple truths,
But on our England's green and pleasant land,
They walk, head up and free..!

BLAIR.
I see you're most affected Cherie,
I'm in agreement with you to the hilt,
So tell you what, the best thing we can do?

CHERIE AND SEC.
Yes? Yes-

BLAIR.
We'll take a little holiday abroad,
In some secluded sunny clime,
Remove ourselves from centre stage,
So no one nags, accuses, or throws slime.
Just gently fly away all quiet like
(I'll keep the mobile on for urgent calls)
But think what bliss to be away,
And let the others take the flack
And with old tubby Prezza left in charge,
There's nothing really anyone can do!
He'll be a caretaker of sorts,
And this will cool things down, deflate
The anguish and the toil In our fair state.

So when were back, so brown and svelte
Will be all calm again and quiet,
So pack the bags my dearest sweet,
And please do not forget to pack,
My favourite swimsuits, they're really neat!

FIXED GRINS AND FADE OUT.

GHOST OF PRIME MINISTERS PAST:
What is a prime minister but a caretaker,
A father figure for our woes,
Dispensing justice, being good,
Listening to our numerous griefs
That we can never ever cure,
But make some small improvements, now and then,
And when we do the world applauds.
Be charming, decent, and, yes, wholesome too;
And if or when it comes to war,
That you reluctantly take on, when,
There is no other choice, then
Fight like hounds, be merciful in victory,
But never ever lie; my God that is the worst,
And drags your reputation in the dirt.
But in the end, no matter what,
No matter just how well you do,
And you've done well, exceeding well,
You've ruled so long, you have become,
Almost a piece of Albion itself.
But people will get tired of you,
The longer that you stay, the more exposed,
The more the People weary of your face,
They've had enough and want a change,
You cannot rule the weather,
Rain or shine, disasters and calamities,
It's part of life, part of our world.
But we all were hated in the end,
And those who longest stayed, hated the most,

And then blamed for everything that fails,
That disappoints, can never do enough.
Your reputation Tone will survive intact,
Perhaps it's time to go and write your book,
Let others take the flack and calm the rage,
Of course you've made some errors, don't we all?
But in the end we do believe,
You did the very best you could,
You really did; you certainly could spin
The words but they came from the heart, we know,
But it's not fair to see you twist and squirm,
Exchanging pieces on your old chess board,
Because it looks like check, old mate,
Or getting pretty close I'd say,
So give yourself a break, go out in style,
There's never been a PM like you Tone,
Nor sadly is there like to be, I think.
You certainly had a flare, a shining eye,
Which makes so many of us look dull as rain
On a grey wet Manchester day.
Just politicians wearing heavy suits,
And spouting weary platitudes,
A PM's shelf time's not that much,
And you've done more than most.
So sometime we must go before
We leave a very bitter taste,
It's painful because we think! What's left!
When powers so intoxicating
Having dominion over life and death.
So take a break and see your mate, your good pal Bush.
Stretch out, enjoy the life you've earned,
You'll have a big space in our history books!
But whether it's good or bad, no one can tell,
But does it really matter; down there in Hell?

UPRISING

Warsaw, Poland, nineteen forty-three,
April the nineteenth... just to be precise,
When Jewish rebels spewed into the street
Their hatred for the murdering Nazi lice.

The few machine guns they had costly bought
Chatted their deadly song into the brutes
Who screeching, fled, leaving many a corpse...
'How could they do this to us, they're only Jews!'

Just lice, vermin, scum, untouchables,
So preached philosophers from their Nazi lairs,
While yelling in dissonant, German, guttural tones,
'Heil Hitler!' and thrust their arm up in the air.

How could the German nation salute this beast?
A nation that spawned Beethoven, Goethe, Bach,
They heard his racists' filth, got on their knees
And cried out 'Mein Führer' from their deepest hearts.

German or Nazi, ah now, that's the rub.
The Nazi mask conceals the inner man,
Those murderers were not Germans, no, not us!
The 'Nazis' did it... Decent Germans ran!

The nation loved him with one mighty mouth,
He built the motorways, made people work,
In Bierkeller or in the Kaffeehaus,
Hitler was sung while dirty yids were cursed.

Their rotten books were piled high in a pyre,
The thoughts of man confused their addled brains,
They hurled their words into a giant fire
All over Europe spread the Nazi stain.

And now the tidal scum reached Poland's shores,
Two million Hebrews lived in harmony,
Amongst the Polish Christians, obeyed the law,
Built theatres, wrote books and played in symphonies.

The poorer lived and worked, sweated and bred,
Some lived in ghettoes, such as they were called,
Four hundred thousand faced certain death
As bricklayers built the Warsaw Ghetto's walls.

Warsaw was the capitol of the Jewish world,
Zionists and Bundists, capitalists and socialists,
Doctors and surgeons, carpenters and dentists,
Teachers and tailors, hear the warning bell!

And so we wait to hear from the Nazi thugs,
September first in thirty-nine they came...
Jackboots, and helmets like dead cold skulls,
In one week they stood at the Warsaw gates.

How they bombed Warsaw day and fearful night,
In twenty bloody corpse-filled days it fell,
A mere fifty thousand dead, man, wife and child,
And thus began the first glimpse inside hell.

The German Nazis carry their hell within,
Transporting their filth to where they set their feet,
Their breath was acid, they belched poison gas,
Their sweat dissolved the plants, on blood they feast.

And now they sniff the warmer Jewish blood...
Bloodhounds well-trained by their master, the maddest
   Hun,

Salivate as they sink their yellow teeth
Into a Semite throat, the chosen ones.

Chosen to be Treblinka's honoured guests,
Sixty miles away the ovens burn,
The chimneys daily pour their filthy smoke,
And belch from gorging too much kosher flesh.

Their heads were shorn, why waste the precious stuff,
It fills a mattress, cushion, swells a chair,
You may be sitting on Sarah's precious curls,
So don't be sentimental, it's only hair!

But first you work, you lazy parasites!
Forced labour for your kindly Nazi hosts,
Long hours, no pay, we'll squeeze the greasy kikes,
For those too old, we'll turn them into ghosts.

For once, Moishe will taste some honest graft,
You can't exploit the Aryan or the goy,
But 'cause we know the Shylock race is smart...
You'll run the entire ghetto for us... Jew boy!

1940

And now a ring was formed around its throat
On November sixteenth, the ghetto sealed,
Four hundred thousand souls were swiftly crushed
As the weaker died, their space was quickly filled.

From every town and village the race was torn,
Leaving behind the memories of long years,
Mothers, husbands, young wives with child unborn
Were crushed into the ghetto with their tears.

Rumours of deportations now are rife,
It's mid July in nineteen forty-two,
Czerniakow, the ghetto's leader, commits suicide,
He cannot get the Nazi quota filled.

Pity those poor Catholics caught in the net,
Who long ago shed off their Hebrew kin,
But Nuremberg laws did say the smell persists
Of their ancient brother's loathsome skin.

But now the Nazi machine is well in place,
It's time now folks to say the last farewell,
Drag your suitcases to the Umschlagplatz
And take a one-way ticket, first class to Hell!

Treblinka, your foul name will never fade,
But shall outlast the very universe,
While cities, empires and dynasties decay,
Your name will be an everlasting curse.

But drag your rubbish to the Umschlagplatz
To make believe you'll need your precious clothes,
A change of underwear, spare shoes and reading glass,
'Excuse me, here, you'll not need those.'

First, 'Transports' take the orphans, they're no use,
Can't make them work in factories and mines,
Their teacher Janusz Korczak knew the truth,
But held their hands until the end of time!

First, take the old and weakest, they're no use,
You have no papers? Then you're next, my friend.
It's just a formality since the Nazi brutes
Have busy ovens, whose hunger never ends.

The canisters of gas they dropped within,
And watched the writhing bodies scream and gasp,
Clawing their way into a human pyramid,
The nearest to the top, they died the last.

'Fight back!' survivors cried, 'What's wrong with us?
Jewish resistance, that will never be.

When four hundred thousand were alive
We marched to death with neat efficiency!'

But now with only fifty thousand left
There was determination to 'resist'...
Three hundred and fifty thousand souls wiped out
Within three months by those who deal in death.

July until September, forty-two,
Civilisation ceases to exist
As transport after transport turned the Jews
Into crushed bones in rancid smoking pits.

A great achievement for the master race,
Which got the tardy trains to run on time,
Inflation cured and euthanasia
For retards and the homosexual swine.

But most of all, you German Nazi dogs,
You did the utter indescribable,
Murdered children, yes even God was shocked,
While your wives ate Sacher Torte and read the Bible.

So now, oh yes, oh now we will begin,
For now, yes now, this truly is the last,
The last time we will pack our suitcases,
And like dumb cattle, walk to railway cars.

No more, no more, the vulture's drunk enough,
An ocean of blood won't slake the monster's thirst,
So now resist those filthy vampire bats,
Our slogan: We will die like humans first!

Fighting, striking, attacking the Nazi curse,
Mordecai will lead the rebel troops,
A Joshua has risen from the earth,
But first we kill those compromising Jews!

To save their frightened skins they aid the beasts.
Such scum has no continuance on this earth,
We must stamp out this vermin with our feet,
Even if we share the self same blood?

These Judases who'd sell their brothers' flesh,
They swooned into the devil's wretched arms,
Descendants of great Moses who then smashed
The tablets, seeing them lick the golden calf.

On January ninth, nineteen forty-three,
Nazi chief Himmler visits the ghetto,
Desiring an opportunity to gloat
At dying remnants and thin walking shadows.

Crawling along the bloodstained ghetto walls,
Freezing on the heartless naked streets,
Just fifty thousand humans left to kill,
'I want eight thousand more to go this week.'

Himmler might be ordering sausages,
But living human sausages at that...
Snap your fingers for Herr Ober... 'Ja,'
'Acht tausend Juden, bitte...' but no fat!

But Mordecai Anielewicz, rebel lord,
Said, 'No one goes... This is no more,
No more, no more, and now this is the law.'
The empty streets were silent when the Nazis came.

Yes, suddenly the rebel guns barked out...
And shattered ancient myths of Nazi might,
They fled like screaming cowards, shitting pants,
Jawohl! The Nazi cowards were put to flight.

Jawohl, jawohl, jawohl, ja fucking wohl!
Brave heroes you are, defenceless girls you rape...

What guts, to drag old women from their homes,
So brave to tear a mother from her babe!

So now eat, homemade steel, pig swine and cry...
How dare the Yiddish bastards dare not die...
How dare they, dare they, dare they, dare they try...
To live like human beings, refuse to die?!

The rebels' action lasted just three days...
But now the end is marked, our days are short,
But the rebels' armed resistance is here to stay,
Outnumbered, that's the way, we always fought.

The weeks they passed, the deportations ceased,
The coward Nazis licked their wounds and watched,
For once the ghetto rebels rejoiced with glee,
For German blood now stained its ancient streets!

The rebels' fighting organisation watched,
And waited eighty-seven days, alert.
Himmler allowed three days to clear the 'rot'...
It took a month and Nazis tasted shit.

April the nineteenth, the Jews' Passover feast,
When death passed over the Israelite slaves,
The blood of the lamb on the doorposts was a sign,
For God's dark angel, who would pass them by.

So on this night we celebrate the flight,
And eat unleavened bread salted with tears,
Remembering the time when mothers gathered mites,
And walked into the desert for forty years.

So on this night we must remember this,
April nineteenth in nineteen forty-three,
The uprising began and rebel fists
Threw hand grenades and slew the enemy!

When Jewish fists were clenched, clenched hard and tight,
Not held up in the air like frightened slaves
Gathered up and marching, a mournful sight,
As listlessly they stumbled to their graves.

But not tonight, not this night, never more.
Now, set this down into the holy scroll,
April nineteenth in nineteen forty-three,
And remember it with heart and soul!

It first began on January eighteen,
We heard the Nazi orchestra begin,
Shouts and gunfire, and trucks and screams,
As Nazis ordered... 'Get out in the streets!'

'Get out! Get out! Be at the assembly point,
A bullet in your head if you don't speed,
I'll bash you black and blue until your joints
Are broken, cracked, and then I'll watch you bleed...'

But Mordecai Anielewicz prepared,
A dozen fighters pistol'd up and brave,
They planned to join the frightened marching herd,
Who tramped down solemn streets like abject slaves.

They had their guns concealed and at a cue,
They stepped out of the line of stumbling Jews,
And turned their weapons on their charming hosts,
Their orders... 'Take the German nearest you!'

The Nazis for the first time were attacked,
Inside the ghetto, their favourite slaughterhouse!
The victims ran, dissolved into the cracks.
The cat was swallowed by the tiny mouse.

Oh joy, oh God, what wonders do we see,
The S.S. killed and wounded, others fled

Leaving their caps and weapons as they flee,
Alas, there were so many rebels dead.

Let's praise dear Yitzhak Zuckerman and his small group,
Fighting with much courage in Zamenhov Street,
The Nazis burst in hungry for those Jews,
Now rats would celebrate the German feast!

The Jewish fighting organisation, so named,
They sprang out from the shadows, just appeared,
They freed those being led to the deathly trains,
Knowing their time was short, they had no fear.

The Nazis whined with fury, sick with rage,
And seized the old, the weak and those infirm,
Not face the strong, the young, they were afraid,
Shame, six thousand more were dragged away.

Mass slaughter of the innocent on that fourth day,
In the ghetto's bloody streets one thousand souls
Were murdered for their gall and so they paid
For not trotting respectfully to their graves!

The January action left the S.S. dazed,
The ghetto now was quiet, not a face,
The Germans hesitate, how could these slaves
Dare to attack the devil's master race?

The devil stunk inside his loathsome hide,
The Jew's example might inspire the Poles,
As news of the resistance spread far and wide,
The Nazis cogitated, there was a lull.

Now the cautious ones in jubilation cheered.
Who once believed resistance would tighten the knot
Of the hangman's noose that sits around their throat,
They wracked themselves 'tween doubt and new found
    hope.

And what a sad success it really was,
Symbolic, a gobspit in the Nazi eye,
Although we scratched the loathsome Hitler beast,
We could not stop those led away to die.

Yet we were mistaken, there was no plan
To exterminate the ghetto to the last man...
Slave labour was still needed by the Hun,
'More uniforms!' as Nazis died in tons...

But the Warsaw ghetto now must be destroyed,
Erased from off old Poland's scar-lined face,
For the Nazis were afraid Der Untermensch,
Would persuade the Polish criminals to be brave.

'Oh no!' the German factory owner shrieked,
Since Yiddish blood was turned to German gold,
'We must not lose the labour that's so cheap,
The Wehrmacht must be fed and product sold!'

There was a bitter conflict for Jew flesh,
The ovens of Treblinka must be filled,
But the Wehrmacht needs the labour, needs their sweat,
But the S.S. orders are 'Take out and kill!'

Five thousand heads a day were put on trains,
From Warsaw to Treblinka, ran on time,
The factories of death through sun and rain,
Producing nothing but an everlasting stain.

A stain that never ever can be erased,
Though centuries will heap their heavy years,
The rancid smell will always dribble through,
Treblinka soil is sodden with blood and tears.

But now in conflict are the wretched Huns,
For their efficiency in killing Jews,

Depleted factory workers making guns,
'Our soldiers die without their killing tools!'

TRANSFER
Friedrich Wilhelm Krüger, S.S. general:
'There are advantages and disadvantages,
'Though Himmler wishes all the Jews expelled,
They are the best mechanics and we pay no wages!

'The lazy Poles cannot do the job as well,
The Reichführer Himmler must then change his mind
Before we consign Yiddish scum to Hell,
Suck out the fruit and throw away the rind.'

Walter Többens, factory owner begs,
'Please, Jews, come to our lovely new location,
Leave the ghetto with its criminal dregs,
We'll teach your children, learn a new vocation.'

But inexplicably, the Jews did doubt
The promises of the German entrepreneur...
Of thirty-six hundred workers, thirty turned out...
The rebels had warned them, 'Do not volunteer!'

Shelters, tunnels and cellars were fortified,
The smell of resistance electrified the air,
The destruction of the Ghetto was in sight,
This time they'd fight like tigers in their lair.

Furiously they dug their holes at night,
A warren of bunkers deep beneath the earth,
Their work was done with skill for the heart was light,
We would see the Jewish rebellion's birth!

Everything was thought of, nothing rushed...
Even sanitary arrangements made,
There must be water and fresh air, food stuff.
Our experts even wired electric cables.

The siege may last for ever, so we need
Doctors, medicines, bandages and yes, cyanide.
And now there was a bunker for us all,
And so we wait, barbarians, make your strike!

The ghetto was a city that was split,
Houses above the ground, tunnels below,
An army of worker ants, they daily teemed,
The Nazis prepared to make their final blow.

PAST
Now we few were the last, the very last,
Three hundred thousand others turned to smoke,
And this is just from Warsaw, the die was cast
To crush us in one final brutal stroke.

Between July and September forty-two,
The Nazis siphoned up the pliant Jews
'Out of your house, right now, or you'll be shot!
Juden, move! Take your belongings, take your rot!

'Take your stinking children, take your bags,
You must have a number, move faster, scum,
March in line! You skeletons in rags,
Faster! March! You shit, move quicker, run!

'We have whips and bayonets for you...
Some will be selected, ja! the special few,
They'll be allowed to be our slaves, you Jews
Have all the luck, let's see if it's you!

'March along the line, no permit, no?
Then head off to the Umschlagplatz... Go!...Go!
What's that under your coat, a baby's cry?
A bayonet thrust will save the kid a ride!'

So some did work and some did swiftly die,
And from Treblinka they flew to paradise,

Yet some escaped and lived to tell their tale,
David Nowodworski describes Hell:

'Even at death's door the Nazis schemed,
To make believe you have a future life,
"Go to the bathhouse, shower and get cleaned,
We will rid you of your crawling lice."'

Met at the station by a welcoming crew,
Alsatian dogs and guns and stinging whips,
So kind of you to greet your fellow Jews,
Our brethren police were executing Yids!

They saw their brethren, dressed in uniform,
Fulfil their roles with added zeal,
Your Jewish brother sheds his brother's gore?
The S.S. forced them, kill or you'll be killed.

'If you do not give us five heads a day,
The quota in the ghetto, never fail,
Your wives and children will make up your pay.'
The tears of angels fell like heavy hail.

But now this is the last, the very last...
The ghetto fighters now were unified,
The final struggle will shortly come to pass,
And Nazis too will join the funeral pyre.

We wait, we wait, so patiently for the time,
Why can't those German Nazis leave us alone?
Always ordering with their shrieking tones,
They want to strip our flesh right to the bone.

It is their cause, the maniacs' contract,
It focuses their minds beyond themselves,
Their vacant souls become a tomb for rats,
And scapegoats make the Nazi bums feel swell.

The enemy must decide the final date,
Which marks for all of us the end of time,
A thousand years in Poland we have made
Our home, and now upon our corpses Fritz will dine.

We did all the things that people like to do,
Sat in cafés and argued about Karl Marx,
Went to the movies, held each other's hands,
Walked on Sunday, fed ducks in the park.

Now huddled in bunkers we talked and analysed,
Ate our basic food, black bread and jam,
Sometimes some soup, a blessing to have rice,
But priority, to arm each precious man.

Of fighting groups there now were twenty-two,
The Dror, Hashomer Hatzaír and the Bund,
The Communists had four trained fighting troops,
Akiva, Godonia, Po'alei and Hazion.

The Ghetto was divided in three states,
The central, where the wretched poor exist,
The workshop area, home for all the slaves,
The brushmakers for the human two-pronged sticks.

Mordecai Anielewicz rules the central state,
Entrenched like Joshua, waiting for his time,
Israel Kanal had eight brave fighting squads,
Commander Yitzhak Zuckerman had nine.

What can we do but fight with heart and soul,
What military experience have we, none?
No hand to hand battles in the street or squares,
Their crushing force will blow us to kingdom come.

What chance against these well-fed, well-armed thugs,
Who leave their warm barracks to kill thin Jews?

At night they shave and shower off our blood,
While we sip slowly on our watery stew.

But like gazelles we'll leap from roof to roof,
From many places surprise the sleeping beast,
From alleyways and crevices we'll shoot,
Wait until they follow, then let your bullets feast!

Sometimes in darkened alley we'll appear,
Or else behind a broken chimney pot,
And then our sweet grenades will swiftly tear
Their hearts out, and then we'll see them drop.

There is no plan for withdrawal, none,
Since this is where we fight and where we die.
'We want to save the honour of mankind,
And rip out of their throats the wicked lie.

That never did we fight back, defend ourselves,
Like frightened sleepwalkers we marched to die,
But now brave friends we fought, and fought back well,
While others gaped, their limp hands by their sides.

Landings, alcoves, basements, corners, roofs,
From all directions fire and never cease,
Ration your precious bullets, only shoot
When you can see the eye of the Nazi beast!

Passover

April nineteenth, nineteen forty-three,
We celebrate Passover, even here,
But tonight be vigilant, do not sleep,
For Pharaoh will rise again, beware!

But then did Moses have the ear of God,
And did he not come forth with miracles?
So we pray this night, 'Strike with thy rod,
Do not be deaf to the cries of Israel!'

'The Germans are coming this night, prepare defence,
Now listen to your standing orders, Jews,
"Jan – Warsaw" is the magic word, good friends,
The password for this night and God save you.'

Get down into the bunkers, block the streets!
Use everything to halt the Nazis' path!
Old furniture in doorways, cupboards, seats!
Your wardrobe, tables, chests and broken glass!

Marek Edelman, commander, the Ghetto's brushmaking
 section,
Reports: 'Information reached them at two A.M.
The Germans are advancing, prepare for action,
Tonight we fight, take your positions, men!'

Oberführer von Sammern-Frankenegg,
Was not expecting too much opposition,
'Ja, a little maybe, from these dregs,
The Yids don't fight, it's not their disposition.'

Yet Himmler had small confidence in him,
So sent his S.S. general Jürgen Stroop...
Against uprisings Stroop knew how to win,
There was no depth to which he would not stoop.

His murder expedition was to earn
The Nazi devil the Iron Cross first class,
Awarded by Field Marshall General Keital
For valour against the helpless human dross.

Two thousand German soldiers, fighting fit,
Machine guns numbering one hundred and thirty-five,
A cannon, flame throwers, thirteen heavy guns,
Twelve hundred rifles and three armoured cars.

Ukrainians and camp guards to go in first,
To take the bullets if they start to fly,

No, this action will not take too long,
We'll smoke them out and, ja, we'll watch them die.

The Jewish fighting force was just in name,
Of military training barely none,
Seven-fifty young combatants and brave,
Desperate to fight and each man had a gun.

Revolvers of various calibres and makes,
Ammunition, ten to fifteen rounds...
Four hand grenades for each, mostly handmade,
And Molotov cocktails make a lovely sound.

A couple of machine guns that they earned
In the January rebellion when they slew
Some Nazis, now their spouting mouths would turn
Upon the enemy when once they spat on Jews.

April the nineteenth at four A.M. they came,
Entering the ghetto's now deserted streets,
The fighters in the bunkers did await
The growing sound of Nazis' marching feet.

It sounds like thousands, marching without end!
A march of death and we would die like flies,
They moved as if to war they're being sent,
How weak we felt against this armoured tide.

But others had a different point of view,
Tuvia Borzykowski recorded this:
'At six A.M. the siege surrounded us,
We had them in our sights, we could not miss!

'We did not wait for them to slaughter us,
From each and every post we showered them
With hails of bullets, hand grenades and bombs,
Our homemade efforts fell with great aplomb!'

Exploded as they should, we were relieved,
The Warsaw Ghetto's uprising has begun!
Their wounded and their dead lay in the streets,
We scurried out and swiftly took their guns.

Oh, how they fled, the frightened Nazi scum,
No longer marching in neat, pompous ranks,
But scattered into groups, to walls they clung,
Or hid like frightened beasts behind their tanks.

Like fruit being tossed from heavy-laden branches
Whose limbs swung back and forth in heaving winds,
So hand grenades were hurled from every vantage,
And death pursued them in the screaming din.

The German Nazis were amazed and stunned,
'Juden haben waffen! Juden haben waffen!' they shout,
The Jews have arms! And how they swiftly run,
And bloody Nazi corpses lay round about.

I, Haim Frymer, stationed at the corner of Zamenhof,
Stood on the balcony, my Mauser cocked,
I fired upon the smoking, shrill compost
Of yelling Nazis, burning tanks and dust.

The air was full of wails and wounded screams,
The Nazi killers were totally unprepared,
This was beyond our wildest, wildest dreams,
Now from Jews the Krauts were running scared!

Diving for cover, pissing in their pants,
They turned around and ran, withdrew,
Then from a house in Muranowski Street,
A rebel flag arose in white and blue.

Not just once the Germans fled but twice!
Mordecai Anielewicz in his journal wrote,

For forty minutes one company faced their might,
The second for six hours stayed at their post.

Nearby, our German 'Schmeisser' fiercely barked,
Our submarine gun that was costly bought,
No sweeter music filled our pounding hearts,
Like Joshua's warriors, our survivors fought.

Please God, come to our aid and fill our cup,
As when the sacred oil on Chanukah
Burned brightly for eight days and then eight nights,
Until the enemy was put to flight.

But now the Polish underground must rise,
Strike! my friends, and give us your support,
Our strength is limited, you must see our plight,
We must not say, that all alone we fought.

Don't watch us from your windows and your doors,
Admiring from a distance as we die...
But cast yourselves among us, help destroy
The enemy, while chaos and confusion fly.

Anielewicz wrote to Yitzhak Zuckerman,
Our representative on the Aryan side,
'We need grenades, explosives, machine guns,'
But the desperately needed weapons never arrived.

Zuckerman begged the Polish underground,
'The time, my friends, is swiftly running out,'
They answered, 'Wait until the Russians strike
The Nazis, that's the time to stage a rout.'

The Nazis in disorder and in shame
Withdrew their badly wounded and their dead,
Screaming accusations, who's to blame?
The S.S. General Stroop becomes their head.

A Nazi tank burst into furious flames.
Two armoured cars by our homemade grenades,
Were halted in their tracks, their driver slain,
Twelve dead and many wounded, God blessed this day!

Oh, how the Nazis whined and how they blamed…
Von Sammern's soldiers simply ran away,
Jawohl, the military defeat would be a stain
Upon the proud and mighty S.S. name!

Von Sammern was dismissed, Stroop took command,
He would show Himmler how to kill the pests,
With heavy arms he would destroy the yids,
Then watch them die inside their burning nests.

And so they hoped, but this was not to be,
Not yet a while as fighters returned fire,
But the rebels' bullets sadly could not now reach
The Nazis and their stronger fighting power.

But still they fought, machine guns now were used
By comrades fighting in the central Ghetto,
Again the Nazi raiders were confused,
As bullets round the burning buildings echo'd.

The Nazis slowly moved just step by step,
Penetrating houses, climbing stairs,
Seeking out the killers in their nest,
But when they found it the birds had disappeared.

Swiftly charging, through attics, underground,
Hiding in bunkers, in the sewage tunnels' stew,
Leaping, darting, swiftly while bullets pound,
Refilling rifles and shooting as they flew.

The Nazis were inflamed, their violence grew,
They scoured the sewers, found five hundred Jews,

These were unarmed and helpless and with children too,
They wanted many thousands more but 'Ach! They'll do!'

As there were not enough to cram the train,
More practical to shoot them on the spot,
Or torch their stinking hovels, burn them alive,
There were no limits on Earth to German wrath.

As if we were in medieval times,
When Jews were burnt in London and in York,
Accused of killing little Christian babes,
Stretching the innocent to make them talk.

Confess to crimes that were insane, obscene,
So they could free themselves of heavy debts,
The Jews were money lenders to the king...
So why not slaughter those bloodsucking pests?

Twentieth April, nineteen forty-three,

A strange calm fell upon the streets that night,
The ghettos' creatures wandered out and spoke
Of such wondrous and amazing sights,
The day the Nazi murderers were smote!

This day will surely mark the end of time,
And from this day the seeds will then be sown,
Fed with the martyrs' blood, upon this day
We'll reap the fruit that we can call our own.

The morning came again as German plagues
Advanced and stormed those houses, bearing flags,
Machine guns and light cannon sprayed
Their venom and rebel leader Leon Rodal fell.

But factory owner Többens squealed, 'Please wait,
And save our valuable machinery,'

He begged the General Stroop to relocate
The assets to a safer territory.

'Then, turn the ghetto into one mass grave!'
Stroop thought this was far more sensible.
'We'll kill the terrorists, some scum we'll save,
To be slaves in our vital industry.'

Three German officers at three P.M.,
White handkerchiefs attached to their lapels,
Called for ceasefire, just an interim,
To persuade shop-workers, come and make a deal.

'Deportation's really not so bad,
Your lives you'll save, your families' as well,
These terrorists are criminals, raving mad,
Trust us, you can believe the lies we tell!'

In spite of this fine offer, few came out,
It seems the Jews could not believe the Hun,
Arbeit macht frei is what they always spout,
But after work? Treblinka's not much fun.

So Stroop begins, the ancient ghettos fall,
And centuries of history will turn to dust,
Blowing up the soul of the Hebrew nation,
Since mass murder is not quite enough.

The Warsaw Daily, the city's underground sheet,
Reported the events amid some pride,
'The war of despair continues in the streets,
Through overwhelming courage, Nazis died.

'Yesterday the Germans celebrated
The day when Satan's evil spawn came forth,
The monster Hitler was born on such a day,
On such a day don't celebrate, but mourn!

'This could be a day for amnesty,
A ritual seen throughout the enlightened world,
When heads of state on birthdays decide to free
Some poor souls from their prison'd misery.

'But here mass slaughter is the birthday treat,
To honour Hitler with this unique gift,
Dead women and children for your special feast,
And thousands rotting in mass graves and pits.

'This heroic struggle has no chance,
The Nazi hangmen are a hundredfold,
More stronger as each day the hordes advance,
We must salute the Jewish guts and soul.'

The Daily Warsaw reports on what it sees,
'In two wars in many battles have I been,
But none as deeply moving as yesterday,
As rebels fought on through stinking smoke and flames.'

Facing field cannon and anti-armour fire,
They throw their precious homemade hand grenades,
The enemy actually turn back and retire,
As from rooftops, rattling machine guns spray!

Appeals were posted yesterday on the streets,
On houses bordering the ghetto walls.
'Poles, please help! Alone do not let us fall!
Long live free Poland... Free Poland for all!'

The Germans shouted through their megaphones,
'Appear, six-thirty at the Umschlagplatz!'
Of course dear Nazis we're as mad as you,
The Nazis waited but no guests turned up.

These women are heroines, stalwart, fierce and mean,
Pouring sulphuric acid on the enemy,

Setting their trucks on fire with gasoline,
An army of Deborahs via villainy!

You know this is the second Jewish war,
The first was pitted against the Roman might,
We need a Josephus Flavius to describe
The horrors taking place, such moving sights.

The Jewish war writ down by Josephus
Lives on throughout two thousand bitter years,
Capturing with his pen the very pulse
Of Jerusalem before it sank in tears.

A Jew bearing an automatic rifle
Is wounded, next moment, a woman is by his side,
Takes over his weapon like a blushing bride,
Swiftly refills the rifle and bullets fly!

Tanks have been destroyed and prisoners taken,
Can you believe that this has come to pass?
The prisoners sweat in fear, their faces ashen,
They released the soldiers but held the S.S. fast.

The city was amazed, astounded, drunk
With joy to see their enemy well kicked
By Yids right up its Nazi arse, it hurt
The bastards, how it made Herr Himmler sick!

It did not fade the second day, no way,
That's what the Nazis hoped - fat chance, - like this
Was just a one-off, just a last display,
Before we humbly raise our hands and walk away.
                                        No way!

The campaign now encompassed every ghetto Jew,
The enemy realised this and moved more tanks,
Eliezer Geller waited with his group,
At Leszno Street and warmly gave them thanks!

A tank was hit and then began to burn,
Into the houses the Nazi forces burst,
Enraged and mad to taste the rebels' blood,
They hacked and shot till they had quenched their thirst.

But now, as if in solidarity,
A Polish rebel group did try to mine
The ghetto wall to let escaping Jews
Get through, but they were hampered by a line…

Of curious spectators, staring bug-eyed,
Like this was just a piece of theatre,
While most in Warsaw continued with their lives,
Went shopping, sat in cafés and sympathised…

They watched from windows, rooftops, what a show!
As deep inside the walls a nation died,
A wretched drama was unfolding slow,
But from their blood a new race will arise!

The Nazi units caught five hundred Jews…
Those fit for work would stay alive – for now,
The rest would go to fill the transport queue
For 'Canada', slang word for 'gas chamber', to you.

Oh, how bravely they fought that second day,
Jacob Rakower – Jewish porter broke through
The siege with ten men to the other side
Carrying Commander Leon Rodal, who sadly died.

Oh, strongly fight, oh you most valiant few,
But when the battle's clearly lost, don't die,
Escape and save yourselves, flee to the woods!
Some did but were betrayed by Polish spies.

But on day four the battle plan had changed,
The fighting had been conducted from fixed posts,

Now they used positions as a base,
From which to leap and then dissolve.

Like hornets we will launch surprise attacks
With smaller mobile groups to pounce and catch
The bastards when they smoke a fag or crap,
Then fly as bullets whistle past our backs.

The bunkers wind like snakes into the earth,
Weaving, twisting, linking the fighters chain,
Providing outlets to the sewer's dirt,
Our sanctuary, where we nurse our sick and maimed.

Now the purveyors of death, the S.S. troops,
Decide with fire that they should burn us out,
The stinking smoke of hell became our day,
And tongues of flame scorched up the sky at night.

We have no burning desire to be burned alive,
The Nazis lit infernos on every side,
The only chance we have, take one long breath
And run, run, run, escape with all your might!

Tracing through the raging, dancing flames
The fighting units file out one by one,
From passageway to passageway and house to house,
To the central ghetto we must run!

There was a narrow opening in the wall,
But guarded by Ukrainians and armoured police,
Our shoes were wrapped in rags to dull their fall,
Oh miracle, we make it to the street!

Now a shout, and then a light snaps on,
Romanowicz blinds it with a well-aimed shot,
The units make it, not losing anyone,
We greet our comrades, whispering 'Thank God'.

Evacuation

Többens, factory owner, gives guarantee,
'The workshop workers are safe, don't join the mob!
It's true we're safe, they need our industry,
Why die in glory, when in time, we may be free?'

Többens grins hard, 'Your permit makes you safe,
That means you're vital for the war machine,
Those without permits will of course be shot,
Come to the Umschlagplatz, Arbeit macht frei!'

Five thousand workers duly assembled there,
We have some concentration camps to choose,
Majdanek, Auschwitz, Mauthausen, Buchenwald,
Which one do you think will have the better view?

But now the S.S. had complete control,
The factory owners had lost their cherished prize,
The workers would be daily worked and flogged,
And at the end, death marches for exercise.

The fourth day of this fierce unequal struggle,
The Nazis now strengthened their vicious grip,
Flame throwers scorched the hideouts of the rebels,
They jumped from windows and fell like broken twigs.

Whole families sometimes wrapped themselves in sheets,
Tied strongly, they descend the burning pyre,
But in the shadows, the emissaries from hell,
Were waiting to fulfil their heart's desire.

Yet the rebel fighters defend the older Jews,
Huddled together in their stinking bunkers,
In Milna Street, the desperate hundred flew
Into their saviour arms, rescued from hunters.

The bunkers now were useless, choked with smoke,
As hundreds, thousands, sought a place to hide,
Wandering desperately in the sleepless night,
With their few possessions by their side.

Breath

Daniel Anielewicz wrote these words so stark:
'Most of us will die sooner or later,
In bunkers thousands are hiding in the dark,
No air or water, surviving just on hate.

'The bunkers became like ovens, roasting flesh,
The houses above burnt down to their foundations,
And searing hell-like heat spread everywhere,
No window, light or water, no salvation.

'I sweat and think of nothing but fresh air,
How simple pleasures become the most divine,
We sit with open mouths within our mine,
Even a candle's tongue we cannot spare.

'We cannot talk, we cannot breathe or eat,
The food supplies are rotted by the mould,
Which ruins the bread and destroys our precious meat,
They say it'll cool down soon, I don't think so.

'Two days ago this house burnt to the ground,
Yet the heat increases every single hour,
We lie there, silent ears alert for sounds,
Of Nazis poking, while beneath we cower.

'Near naked now but now, nobody cares,
Oh God, some water, please, and a little breeze,
Let's dream of walking in the fresh spring air,
And sitting in cafés and drinking teas...

'Some wretch went crazy, dehydrated, insane,
Crawled to the entrance, moved the hidden cover,
Gulped down the air just like it was champagne,
This could be our suicide, my brother.'

The entire ghetto now was set ablaze,
Oh, how much more, how much more can we take?
Thousands near physical and mental collapse,
We are deserted even by the rats!

When a bunker was by chance discovered,
And the Nazis shout out to surrender,
We say farewell to our friends and lovers
And give the swines some bullets to remember.

Death

April twenty-third, the uprising's fifth day,
General Stroop, convinced the end's in sight,
Mission must be accomplished by sixteen hundred hours.
But the Jews won't surrender, those parasites!

Still hiding in bunkers, in the sewers' shit,
Crawling through broken pipes, sleeping in pits,
Hiding under corpses for the cemetery,
Oh life, how desperately we cling to thee…

April twenty-fifth, it was the seventh day,
'Set fire to the bunkers! Roast them alive!
Blow the damn things up, force them from their sties,
Break! Smash! Kill! Burn! Yes! This is our way!'

Sixteen hundred and ninety caught today,
Two hundred and seventy-four shot, others died in the
    flames,
Till sundown the Nazis worked with utmost zeal,
Mein Gott! They really earn their bloody pay!

April 26th

For days we rot in darkness, thirst and heat,
Hearing only sounds above our heads
Of Nazi shouts and heavy stamping feet,
We cannot move, and slowly wait for death.

We sit and dream of mothers, brothers, girls,
Of life before this nightmare came,
Before the raging sickness of the world
Descended upon us, turning all insane.

If only we had just some minutes more,
We know the Russian army would be here...
They'd sink their teeth into these beasts,
These aliens from another sphere.

Not human beings but something dead and cold,
Vicious, unfeeling, lacking any soul,
Barbarians, stupid, such a Philistine breed,
Why, in Germany, did the devil drop his seed?!

Not yet, not yet, we are not dead, not yet,
From blown-up bunkers we're too weak to crawl,
So shoot us in our pleasant unmarked graves,
We cannot even stand, but we can pray.

Like Midas, Stroop counts his killed and captured prey,
Now nearly thirty thousand and many more today,
Some throw themselves from windows, shouting out their
    curse,
'I shit on Hitler, you bastard!' then their skulls burst.

Mila Five

Scene of bitter struggle at Mila Five,
Germans surround the house, demand we fly,

No answer, so they bomb the house to flames,
The devils wish to see us burned alive.

Germans on one side, the other a sea of flames,
We dash into the courtyard, our fighters gather there,
'Please God, they'll find a way, these young and brave,
Please listen to us carefully, don't despair...'

The only solution, must dash through the flames,
While shooting at the enemy, okay?
'We'll go first'... The bullets flew like rain,
We reached the other side, the Nazis didn't stay!

Unwilling to do combat, the Krauts had fled.
They dare not fight, with those who would risk all!
Flames licked our heads as through the flames we dashed,
Singed faces, hair and clothes, we're through the wall!

Leszno.

Six ten A.M. with tanks taking the lead,
The hearty singing of soldiers march along,
Accompanied by a band can you believe,
Puffed with pride they strut to the military song.

But from Leszno Street another song was heard,
The beat of Molotov cocktails and grenades,
Now the soldiers danced to a different tune,
As Germans fell, they waltzed into their graves!

Survivor Felix Olar verifies:

'We sent a hail of bullets and grenades,
The street echo'd with shouts and shrieks and moans,
Our side fought in every possible way,
The girls replaced grenades we threw like stones.

'Like stones upon a riverbank we'd play,
"See who can hit that distant bottle first",
That's how we used to waste a summer's day,
By throwing stones, but now the Nazis cursed!

'Brave girls, they showed no fear, they looked so calm,
Ready to die honourably on the spot,
They came and went, no sound, no tears,
Their soothing presence was to us a balm.'

Young rebel fighter, Dorka Goldkorn writes,
'I was in the Smocza sector at the time,
We jumped for joy, we saw the tank in flames,
The most beautiful moment of our lives!

From a window, two men and a woman lean,
Dishevelled, faces blackened, their clothes on fire,
Laughing Germans photograph the 'scene',
The victims hurl themselves to Earth, and slowly expire.

No-one offers assistance to quench the flames,
Just the mocking laughter of spectators,
The smell of blood intoxicates their brains,
Sated at last, they march off singing, elated.

Mordecai Anielewicz to the Aryan side

Have you sent food packages? (Read: weapons)
Don't forget our eggs, (homemade grenades)
The kids would love some candy (send some bullets)
And don't forget salami (we need revolvers).

Michalek, alias Henjek Kleinweiss,
Ghetto product and abandoned child,
He lived by selling lemonade in the street,
A soul spawned in the slums and running wild.

Joined the rebels, courageous, intelligent and agile,
Quickly mastered the use of arms, his skills
Were needed, escort a woman to the other side,
But they were captured to be deported or killed.

Shrewd Michalek told the officers, 'Hey, wait,
I know about some bunkers right nearby,
You want to make a deal, I'll give you Jews,'
His captors followed eagerly the lie.

On entering a passageway he pounced,
With lightning speed he snatched the Nazi's gun,
And shot him swiftly dead... and then he flew.
The other Nazis were amazed and stunned.

Before they could recover, Michalek reappears,
Slays two more Germans and then speeds off again,
Michalek's cunning cost the Germans dear,
In battle the young hero met his end.

Ghettograd!

April the twenty-seventh: it's now nine days!
The Jewish fighting organisation survives,
As one limb dies, new branches take their place,
It strikes the enemy each and every way.

Partisan tactics comrades, not just defence,
We hunt the hunters now and make our kill,
The Polish people clap and are impressed,
We need your help, my friends, not just good will.

They like to call the ghetto 'Ghettograd',
In honour of the famous Russian siege,
But they had armies racing to their help,
Who helps us as we helplessly bleed?!

No supporters from the outside world
To rescue the dying Ghetto, only words,
People in England and the U.S. cannot see,
For if you did, your eyes would not believe.

Such horrible crimes beyond your comprehension,
Yes, people are dying in this filthy war,
But not like this, against wild beasts of prey,
Whose poisoned minds obey no moral law!

Yes, you have armies, brave soldiers who die,
But we here die in different ways,
Unarmed women and children burned alive,
By laughing hyenas, relishing the slain.

The ghetto must not vanish without a trace,
For all that is courageous would vanish too,
The smoke clouds over the ghetto are a disgrace,
If all you can do is watch and sit and wait!

'Poles, stop informing on the Warsaw Jews!
Put an end to this practice which defiles our name,
Stop handing them over to our enemy!
Christians, remember, Christ did not die in vain!'

Wladyslaw Sikorski, the Polish leader writes,
'The greatest crime in history is taking place,
Assist the tortured Jews, much as you can,
I beg you, show our friends a human face.'

Lest they believe the entire world had died,
For who can watch this crime and not shout out,
'Stop your criminal act of genocide,
You are less than humans, less than dogs!'

Stop it! You race of murderers, Satan's spawn,
Stop it! For you will never again be a nation,

Stop it! Your children will wish never to have been born,
Than admit 'My parents were of that generation!'

'I'm sorry, we sympathise, not much we can do,
Collaboration is impossible, I'm afraid,
We have to choose the right moment to move,
Not be driven by emotion on the day.'

'We watch from our balconies, a frightful sight!
Yes, we do eat, not a shortage of food,
Those thunderous echoes keep us awake at night.
But we must keep silent or they'll come for us too!'

The wall has two sides

'Wherever there is a war come the hyenas,
Sniffing to exploit the helpless Jew,
Our pathetic friends who are in hiding,
These evil ones are fortunately the few.'

The Polish race is moral, upright and Christian,
Charitable and decent in their lives,
But others in the Polish police are vicious,
Corrupt, they merge themselves with Nazi slime.

Sunday, April twenty-fifth was Eastertime,
Holidaymakers dress in gay attire,
The carousel turned and Polish spirits were light,
As a loathsome pall rose in the Warsaw sky.

There were hawkers of sweets and even cigarettes,
And music filled the square and cannon boomed,
Such a beautiful Sunday, flowers in girls' hair,
As burning victims painfully expired.

Behind the wall the carousel is heard,
A child is cradled in her mother's arms,

Do you ask, dear mother, why you are in hell,
While other children are dancing free from harm?

Stiffening corpses scattered in the broken streets,
Stared at by Ukrainian volunteers,
Stockings torn, shoes still on your feet,
You might be resting, dreaming away your fears.

Who knew your name? You led a full life once,
You had a purse with house keys and small change,
Bought cat food, and made delicious potato cakes,
Put plasters on your daughter when she fell.

Who knew your name? You led a full life once,
Laughed at Charlie Chaplin, wasn't he funny?
Stared in shop windows, Fridays washed your hair,
And picnicked by the river on a Sunday.

Who knew your name? You led a full life once,
The breakfast cooked and ready at eight A.M.,
Sat and cut the cloth, lapels so finely stitched,
Returned at six and did homework for the kids.

Who knew your name? You led a full life once,
Each night your pretty daughter practised scales,
You got on buses, wrote letters to aunts,
Each Friday morning bought a chicken without fail.

'Stand the bunker captives against a wall,
Reveal where other bunkers are, you Jews.
A bullet through your head or clemency,
You choose, they gave us many bunkers more.

'Okay, Jew, speak in Yiddish to your friends,
Tell them be smart and leave now in one mass,
Or else we'll blow the bunker to little shreds,
No answer? What about a taste of gas?

'Oh, watch them stagger out, sick, choking, blind...
My God, like smoking out some dirty rats,
You should have come out, Jews, when we were kind,
Now drag your carcass to the Umschlagplatz.'

'A splendid catch today', the general writes,
Each day of course he keeps detailed reports,
Sixteen hundred and fifty-five Jews were caught,
One hundred and ten shot, the rest... Transport!

May First

The stupid Yids won't leave without brute force,
So now we bomb the bloody sewage canals,
One fifty Jews escaped to the Aryan side,
Shot on the spot by police, with hunters' eyes.

May the third, the fight continues on,
Five hundred soldiers purge and search the ruins,
Each day our numbers are reduced as we succumb
To bombs, explosives, guard dogs and gas fumes.

We leave our burrows with its air so foul,
We stumble blinded by the sudden light,
We hear jackbooted soldiers shouting, 'Raus! Raus!'
We see the broken streets, our eyes are down.

We cannot lift our heads to see...
We collapse outside the bunkers wearily,
A woman gently holds her husband's face,
We now must wait for what will be our fate.

May third, thirty Franciskanska Street,
Seventeen-year-old Shanan Lent was killed,
At twenty-three, Zippora Lehrer fell,
And half the Jewish fighters' blood was spilled.

Mila Eighteen

A new sanctuary is found, Mila Eighteen,
Three hundred hunted Jews found haven there,
A well constructed bunker made by thieves,
This was the criminals' and smugglers' lair.

Now rebel commanders, Zionists, communists too,
Link up with gangsters and society's rogues,
Since blood links us to every single Jew,
Now all are allies 'gainst the common foe.

The bunker was enormous, three long blocks,
Dug deep into the earth like mythic beasts,
Lived there with creatures of the underworld,
But now we hear the tread of Nazi feet.

Always scrabbling in the burning embers,
Digging out starved or lifeless, dying Jews,
Why can't you maniacs leave us now in peace?
Go fight your losing war instead, leave us our few!

Shmuel Asher was the king of Mila Eighteen,
From the bowels of the earth he rules,
Smuggling bread and liquor through the sewers' lanes,
'Your subjects would go through fire and water for you.'

They were our guides by day and smoking night,
Like supple cats they'd crawl and jump the ruins,
So we could keep an eye on the German might,
Who from our hate are not so quite immune.

Not any more, we pick and choose to strike,
We scratch the gruesome monster here and there,
Had we a sharpened, deep and long steel knife,
We'd cut its jugular inside its lair.

Alas, on May the eighth the Nazis came,
'Everyone outside!' the familiar shriek,
As they surrounded the bunker, Mila Eighteen,
The rogues obeyed, but the fighters clenched their teeth.

The Germans injected gas, threw hand grenades,
The fighters gasping, still returned the fire,
Soon the rebels began to suffocate,
'Is it not better to die when we desire?'

'Let us give our lives back to our Lord,
Believe me, this is the noblest way to go.
By our own hands, than falling into theirs,
We fought a brave fight,' they answered, 'Let it be so.'

Let it be so and yes, let it be so,
As in Masada so it shall be here,
Each one took the gun for their own head,
Mila Eighteen became a memorial for the dead.

Thus ended the lives of a brave heroic group
Of courage, determination without fear,
Who inspired the Ghetto Jews to strike, rebel,
We will remember you till the end of years.

The lights are going out all over Europe,
Soon there will be darkness, cold and death,
Wherever these Barbarians tread, the hope
For humanity is sucked out with its breath.

But still, even now the battle does not end,
As bunkers are destroyed, we hide in holes,
As holes blown up in sewers, so the dregs
Of humankind still dare to live and hope.

Hope that the world outside must see this crime,
Beyond all crimes in bloodstained human history,

Beyond imagination, beyond belief,
To rip an ancient race from off the earth.

Non-combatants, civilians, women, children,
Innocent, unprepared, old people, sick...
Pregnant women and even babes in arms
Snatched from their nursing mother's teats.

May the twelfth, thirty more bunkers found.
Six hundred sixty-three more wretched Jews,
Sent to Treblinka where time always stops,
But those who couldn't make the train were shot.

May sixteenth, to celebrate the end
Of this victorious and murdering spree,
Stroop blows up the ancient synagogue
To emulate his Roman ancestry.

When Romans destroyed Jerusalem's holy temple,
For that the seeds of their downfall were sown,
 Stroop too will have his monument in time,
A dangling corpse, at the end of the gallow's rope!

Shmuel Zygelbojm, an activist -
Exiled in London, friends nearly all dead,
Each day he cried for western action,
To the American military he passionately begs...

'Save the Warsaw Jews!' 'We don't have time!'

Each day, each minute, another person dies,
Each word I speak, another life is shed,
Each breath I take they suck a human life,
Each heartbeat stops another's heartbeat dead.

'To save the Jews, we really don't have time,
You see the allied war machine is set,

I know the principle is really fine,
But our plans are made, we cannot change the text.'

Zygelbojm knew the ghetto was dying fast,
So he chose to die a fighter with his friends,
On May thirteenth, before the British parliament,
He set himself alight and said, 'Amen'.

'For these evil acts the blame does lie
On all mankind who turned their face away,
No real effort was made to stop this crime...
A hand extended would have saved much pain.

'I cannot be silent for my murdered race,
With their weapons in their hands my dear friends fell,
I cannot die with them I am sad to say,
But throw my ashes please, in their mass grave.'

The accountant Scroop takes up his month's account,
Seven thousand Jews were wiped out on the spot,
Six thousand nine hundred transported to Treblinka,
A handsome profit for a tiny loss.

Six hundred thirty-one bunkers were destroyed,
And that filthy ghetto burnt to the ground,
Even the synagogue exists no more,
But anyway, they'd have no customers now!

But the ghetto's light has not been quite snuffed out,
Something's moving in the broken earth,
The heart still beats and creatures stir at night,
No German dares enter until the morning light.

As if the Golem has awoken here,
The monster created by the Jews of Prague
To take revenge against the enemy,
And protect the old community from harm.

Stirrings in the tunnels of the earth,
The blood pours through, the heart still beats,
The hands still clench, the mouth still eats,
The eyes still see, the head still thinks.

Hundreds are still left alive who fight,
Taut faces, sucked-in cheeks, half-crazed,
The ghetto now belongs to us,
We still have plenty of those hand grenades.

May 26th

Survivor Arieh Neiberg's diary says,
'Women and children were lying in pools of blood,
We stare at the tangle of arms and legs,
Just minutes earlier these were living flesh.

'We stand in grief, cannot hold back our tears,
A corpse begins to move, to come to life,
A child no more than seven, blindfolded, cries,
"Jews, please find us water, have no fear…"

'Another child she gathers up from off the ground,
Also alive, not even wounded, maybe five,
They quench their thirst, the words they tumble out,
"I'm Irka Rubenstein, she's Halinka Eisenstadt."

'The Germans took us from the bunker,
"Take off your clothes," they said, a search was made,
All afternoon we stood there, cold and naked,
By night we would be killed unless we betray…

'Our families in the bunkers, we were afraid,
So someone volunteered, was led away,
The rest of us were killed and then we fell
Upon the ground, and there I lay quite still.

'"When you hear the shooting," my mother said,
"Fall quickly on the ground and do not move."
I tried not to breathe when I was kicked,
So they'd believe that I was really dead.

'Then they left and marched off loudly singing,
My mother's body protected me from them,
Since her warm blood on top of me was flowing,
And so she saved me even in her death.

'By chance I stepped on Halinka's little foot,
It moved! I felt her pulse, the heart still beats!
We heard some voices, the killers returned I thought,
We lay there frozen, for the guns retort.

'But then we heard your voices in our tongue,
Oh what relief, it's safe, these men have gone,
My mother's dead, I kissed her cheek goodbye,
Why do they do these things, please, tell me, why?'

June

We cannot do the things that people do,
We cannot wash our clothes or brush our teeth,
We cannot shave our beards or cut our hair,
We cannot walk and breathe the sweet fresh air.

We cannot make some tea or boil an egg,
We cannot eat some fruit or even bread,
We cannot sleep inside a warm, soft bed,
We cannot call a friend, our friends are dead!

One day decided to collect the rain,
Put out a series of broken pots to claim
The precious fall of heaven's liquid silk,
We'd never know again thirst's awful pain!

September 25th, 1943

Of forty-five that made our special group,
Just four remained alive or only just,
Starvation bloats poor Zamsz's lovely wife,
Shorshan prays each day to God, he must.

'There's nothing else inside his life but faith,
My body's swelling too, let's go to the wall!
Let's go to the Polish side, escape we must,
And if we fail, a bullet will solve all.'

Bricks, April 19th, 1944

And now thousands of Polish working men
Collect the bricks each day, millions of them,
Brick by brick they shift and heave and sweat,
And cart our world away in trucks!

Bricks, bricks, millions of ancient bricks...
Bricks that were our silent bedroom walls,
Bricks that heard our lovemaking and cries,
Bricks that carry the memories of our lives.

Twenty-two and a half million bricks!
Thus the Ghetto exists now in the mind,
Or reconfigured to another place,
In houses, office blocks or factories.

Put your ear to that piece of grimy brick,
That nice extension to your garden wall,
Just as the sea whispers to you in shells,
Do you hear the sobbing cries from Hell?

But now the shreds and shards of Jewish life
That still somehow exist, a shattered urn,
We must escape into the Polish side,
Can we put the splinters back again?

Eliezer Geller made good his bold flight,
Along with all his desperate brave comrades,
The fighter Aaron Carmi also made
The tunnel journey to the Aryan side.

'We made a plan, informed our Polish allies,
One by one we squirmed the tunnel's length,
Then helped each other ascend into the night,
We expected Polish rebels, well-armed men...

'A truck to take us to the forest,
Oh, smell that air and feed our starving guts!
But surfacing into the misty night,
We found not a bloody soul in sight!'

So back and forth and always back and forth
The fighters went, the guide returned to fetch
Remaining Jews who crawled through the sewer's stench,
Dreaming of life after living so long with death.

So tiring, dangerous and difficult to find,
The tunnel rose and fell, split up, which way?
One tunnel leads out to the outer world,
The others, ancient sewers lead to dismay.

Alas, too late the rescue mission starts,
A day too late for Mila Eighteen's guests,
For they themselves had made their peace with God,
But we must save the fighters that are left.

So now again within the stifling tunnel,
More desperate bodies clawed and groped their way,
But now the sun is rising, informer's eyes
Are watching, hoping to nail some Jews this day!

At last the rebels found the tunnel's end,
Breathed deep, replaced the cover on the wound,

A Polish passer-by would see black faces,
Emerging like demons from the bowels of Hell.

But now the realisation struck them hard,
That fifteen people had been left behind,
Go back, go back, too late, the German guard
Now eagerly watched, and just bided his time.

Watched for the lid to move just like
A hungry cat will stalk the mouse's hole,
Waiting with sharpened claws to make its strike,
Alas, no one survived, no, not a soul.

So from Warsaw's four hundred thousand Jews,
Twenty thousand are still alive and hiding,
Honourable Poles help and risk their lives,
God blesses you for every soul surviving...

Joseph Goebbels was indeed amazed,
'These ghetto Jews rebelled, with arms attacked!
Even issue daily military bulletins!
This emphasises what you can expect...

'From Jews when they have weapons in their hands.
God knows,' he said, 'how they obtained these arms.'
Thus spoke the 'voice' of the Nazi nation's man,
For 'God' did know only too well the plan.

As God would see the serpent's wagging tongue,
Stilled two years hence with all his rotten seed,
Poisoned by his own venom, the crippled beast
Was torched, but even fire resisted the doubtful feast.

The Warsaw governor, Dr Ludwig Fischer,
How came he by that doctorate we ask?
Did he tear it from a suckling babe,
Or rip it from the stomach of an ape?

How can a Nazi dog bear such a title
When preaching murder, violence and hate?
Inspiring the Polish population to kill
Any Jew they see who has escaped.

Obergruppenführer Dr Kaltenbrunner,
In Krakow May thirty-first, nineteen forty-three,
Asks, 'Why this preoccupation with the Jews?
The foreign press believe that Nazis stink!

'Is this a noble attribute you think,
That the German nation is seen as cruel,
Killing innocent people because they think
In a different way to us in school?'

But the ghetto's uprising uprose the hearts
And minds of men and women everywhere,
Survivors, prisoners, those in concentration camps,
In east and west became one fighting band.

Treblinka next, the German slaughterhouse,
The factory of death, its proudest mark,
Run with grim Deutschland efficiency,
The gas chambers, your bloodstained coat of arms!

But now inspired, Jews rose against their killers,
Destroyed the camp, and wrecked their damned machines,
No more the image of the passive Jew,
Now the transformation shall begin, anew!

No more, no more the passive pious one...
Since evil breeds where it can feel no fear,
And preys on those who turn the other cheek,
So die a hero's death, not of the meek!

Resist, always resist, defend your lives,
For there will always be insane regimes,

Where morality and justice fly,
And murder ensures a place in paradise.

For all those who fell, the many millions dead,
For all those brutally slaughtered in cold blood,
The heroes who tragically died so we may live,
We bless your souls, and each hair on your heads.

We bless you with everything we have,
Our tears, our blood, our prayers, our hearts,
For you showed us the way to be a human,
Brave, courageous, honourable and ever a part...

Of history's great legends, when the few
Did stand firm as a rock, cower no more,
You Warsaw heroes rest in blessed peace,
Your stars shine bright for ever, oh yes, be sure!

When the war was over, nobody could recognise even one
street in the ghetto, but a hole was indeed found where
Mila 18 once stood; they took a great black stone and
placed it in the space where there was once the house. In
three languages was written: Here on May 8th, 1943,
Mordecai Anielewicz, commander of the Warsaw Ghetto
Uprising, together with dozens of his fighters fell in the
campaign against the Nazi enemy. He was 24.

REQUIEM FOR GROUND ZERO

September eleventh at eight forty-five a.m.
Blue skied Tuesday except for two great birds
Innocently floating on the wide azure.
The morning wakes with coffee cups and eggs.

Men kiss their wives goodbye and get on trains
At towns with funny names like Poughkeepsie,
Nodding their heads to tunes wrapped round their brains,
While staring into the Hudson's glassy stream.

Two silver birds but now with sharpened claws
Are slowly drifting on the endless day,
Craving to tear and feast with bloody jaws
On the innocent unknowing human prey.

And now the early fireman pours his cream
Over his frostie cornflakes, TV blares,
The slow familiar sounds, the children scream,
Before he hits the street he strokes her hair...

As if to say, this piece of earth is mine,
She is familiar with the ritual
Cause like he really thinks his wife's divine,
For her he is the greatest, sweetest pal.

Meanwhile the eye of heaven shines so bright
As Romeo says of his beloved Juliet,
The sun glints off the towers' steel-clad might,
And swarthy men with knives begin to sweat.

Manhattan's lumbering beast wakes up and yawns
And a million diners pour their juice

Into the city's vast collective jaw.
But just before the lip meets heavy cup...

Just before the subway rumbles on
The sour intestines of the monster's gut,
Digesting its human cargo then shat out,
And dog walkers are exercising mut

Just before a man called Roko Camaj,
A window cleaner who wiped the tower's eyes
So it might clearly see the silver bird
And with his chamois leather made them shine...

Just before you finished your second cup,
Eggs over easy and a slice of ham,
Nineteen assassins quietly said their prayers,
Mohammed Atta tied on his red band.

Mohammed Atta sits first class, in seat 8D,
Was so familiar with this one bird's flight,
As New York's patchwork slowly drifts beneath,
He checks his blades and views familiar sights.

But this man had a view inside his head,
To swiftly sacrifice the stewardess.
Before you left a dollar tip and fled,
Hot jets of blood would spurt from her poor neck.

But soon, he will be sat in paradise,
A hundred virgins bubbling at his feet,
Staring at him with adoring tender eyes
For being such a hero, what a guy!

Those two great brazen icons to the gods,
Those stainless mighty phalluses of steel
Where ten thousand worship every day,
One hundred and ten floors up, you can see God's heel.

Computers buzzed and hummed with happy moans
As billions raced across the glittering screen,
Greedily sucking the dollars up for Dow Jones,
'Decaffeinated coffee please, with cream...'

Mohammed Atta sits in seat 8D,
Correctly orders his final Muslim feast.
American Airlines to Los Angeles,
He would have had some fun on Venice Beach.

He might indeed have seen a way of life...
They're not all movie stars and bloated rich,
Could hire a pair of rollerblades and skate
All wobbling along the Pacific Ocean's lisp.

But he had other burning raging thoughts
That churned around his fevered angry brain.
He hates the burger-chewing USA,
Contrasted with the middle eastern stain...

The filthy squalor of the Gaza Strip,
The broken dusty streets and flies and heat,
Long lines of depressed Arabs queue all day
Just for some shitty labouring work, to eat.

But what has that to do with Roko here?
He's just a window cleaner cleaning eyes
Of skyscrapers to make the light so clear;
He didn't want to go to Paradise.

He has his paradise on earth, my friend,
My killer sitting first class, in 8D.
What gives you the right to make his end?
Your God or something, your destiny?

A Boeing 767 surfs the skies,
Floats serenely on the crystal air,

But soon the thousand will see paradise;
Mohammed Atta, lord of deep despair.

We feel, we know, we sense the endless pain
Of roofless souls and wide-eyed children's thirst,
And futile listless refugees, the maimed,
Looking to us all for charity.

Yet nowhere does a people give so much,
Digs deep into their pockets and thrusts out.
No Yankee finds it hard to give a buck,
The world's refuse came here with open mouths.

The poor, the misbegotten, and the Jews
Came running down the gangplank, kissed the ground,
Sweated their guts out, but they earned their dues,
It took a few score years before they found...

A decent place to live on Brighton Beach,
Where delicatessens serve you borscht and lox
And ancient kibitzers sit there and they preach
Free enterprise is better than Karl Marx

Their children then became Americans,
Worked day and night and took home proud degrees.
They lost the accent but enjoyed the nosh,
And so they earned big bucks in Mammon Street.

Those towers sucked up the best brains in the world,
The genius of mankind came here to pray.
One hundred and ten floors up they'd whirl;
The lift ascended to heaven on that bright day...

Brad Sweeney, former naval pilot ace
Travels on United One Seven Five,
His mobile phone collects his final words,
The last ones he would speak before he dies...

'Hey Jules... It's Brad, I'm on a plane...' he said,
'That's just been hijacked; doesn't look good,' he adds.
'Just want to tell you how much I love you...' then
Added these words that were so deeply sad...

'I hope that I call you again,' he said,
'But if not, I want you to have some fun.'
'I want you to live your life' – the sun turned red
'I know I'll see you someday' – the killers won.

What goes through the hearts and minds of men
In times of mighty stress when all the world
Is stripped totally bare right to its core
And when your past before you just unfurls.

Those final moments must be filled with love,
Sublime, most sacred, unequivocal...
Love fills you full to overflow as if
It were your lifebuoy to another world.

As if it was your raft to distant shores
As if it would sustain you far beyond.
Brad Sweeney had just eight long minutes more;
He locked inside his heart those precious bonds.

What goes through the heart and mind of a woman
When returning home from work she sees
A message blinking on the answerphone:
'Hi, honey, sorry, I won't be home for tea!'

She hears his living breathing static words
Across the cold, vast solitary space.
She cannot bear to listen more, it hurts;
But dreams each night of his so-loving face.

Julie Sweeney mourns her husband man
Whose words are caught forevermore on tape;
The last eight minutes when his love did flow
Across the blue and perfect autumn day.

For some of us the shock was far too great;
New York for me's a childhood fantasy...
It's George Gershwin, Bernstein's *On the Town*,
West Side Story or it's *Chorus Line*!

It's Yankee Stadium or corned beef on rye,
Carnegie Hall or Shakespeare in the Park,
Scrapers leaping boldly into the sky...
How could you hurt a city with a heart?

Your bitter twisted minds and poisoned souls,
Your blood so black as evil witches bile,
You cannot kill the innocent parts of man
To cure a body full of festering boils.

From innocent blood you cannot make a home;
The Palestinians will have a state;
Two thousand aching years the Jews did roam;
They also bleed for all mankind enslaved.

We're not insensible to your wounds, your sores,
Each race, each group, each hungry child that cries
For want of a better life came to these shores,
They poured upon this land with every tide.

Do not blame us for all and every grief,
You helped to make your suffering bed of woe
With fundamentalist insanities
Like God is mankind's unforgiving foe.

'American Airlines flight eleven now
Ready for boarding,' the announcer rasps,
No smoking in the bars, nor anywhere,
As overweight yankees gamely waddle past.

Meanwhile, my world goes on in London town,
Serenity and yellow fading stone,

The British Museum has lost its charm
And every ear is glued to mobile phones.

By chance, that night, our play's the death of Christ,
I take a needed break to rest my bones,
I switch the TV on to kill the time
And watch time killed in screams and horrid moans.

I now stand up transfixed, I see it 'live',
I heard the words before the vision came,
I saw the flaming tower forever seared
Into my numb and unbelieving brain.

But no, it's not yet over, this evil game,
'Oh no! Oh no!' The shrieks rang fiercely out;
As into our hearts they flew the second plane,
No accident, of this now we had no doubt...

They like to call us enemies of Allah,
How easily they use the name of God
As if they cleansed their filthy ulcered tongues
In the holy water of the font.

Oh how we love to use the word of God,
As if he was our personal bodyguard,
We spew his name out like we're pushing drugs
And murder is his personal calling card.

We know God weeps for all her souls who die
Before their rightful, fruitful years are spent,
Before two lovers consummate their joy,
God hates to see his treasures torn and rent...

Before the old man fixed the kitchen shelves,
Before his wife had cooked the evening meal,
Before the writer penned his final word,
Before the banker stamped the money deal...

Before the fireman paid the final cheque
Upon his proud and gleaming motorbike,
Before the cop decided to retire,
Before Pete Hanson's wife and daughter died.

Inside United Flight One Seven Five
He called his parents just before the hit,
'Hi Ma and Pa, I think we're going down,
But please don't fret; it's going to be quick.'

Please don't be sick, don't wish to cut your wrists,
Don't heave yourself into each other's arms.
Don't scream or tear your hair nor go insane,
Just weep alone, for this will be your balm.

For tears are heaven's rain to wash away
The filth and dirt and all the rotten pain,
And tears are your own river; upon this stream
Will float your darling precious ones again.

So then it turned, it turned back from the west,
A different pair of hands were on the wheel,
Not John Ogonowski – of pilots, the very best,
But grim-faced death in whom your fate is sealed.

Now dirty hands will guide this silver bird,
This wondrous and most awesome thing of steel,
And this, beauteous miracle of man
Will be in his foul hands, a thing of ill.

And so it turned, it turned back from the west,
It banked sharp left and made down that same stream.
The Hudson showed its shadow on its breast,
And now LA would be a distant dream.

It turned towards two gleaming giant pillars
That even a Samson could not topple down
Death requested a flight path and the killers
Began their killing jamboree, their fun.

'Fun?' you say, yes fun, the greatest fun
Is satisfying your most cherished wish,
Fulfilling your destiny, the father's son
Is sending infidels to the abyss.

And now you hope to sit on Allah's lap
Be bounced and patted on your bloodstained head
Your cheeks be pinched and virgins stroke your feet
As Mary did for Jesus while she wept.

John Ogonowski rose early that day,
Guiding his silver bird so gracefully.
Flight eleven all the way to LA,
Sit back, relax, the pilot knows his way.

'Are you having lunch with us today?'
The stewardess makes her routine programmed chat.
Laptops are out and smart guys check the rates,
The killer's pulse is racing, pit a pat!

Now thumping harder, heart about to burst,
Unzips hand luggage, bares the deadly blades,
Poor stewardess is slashed, oh why should she be cursed?
Her screams bring John Ogonowski, man so brave.

OK, we kill the pilot, take the reins,
This great big silver bird so safely made,
To carry its precious load within its craw,
While you watch movies and the children play.

What is fate? Something that points at you...
From birth maybe; I could be there, yes, me;
I travelled on those routes, I always flew,
Does fate select us for our destiny?

For all those fated on that 747,
Huddled, waiting, unsure for the end

But hoping, I wonder if there's really heaven?
But leave a message just in case, 'I love you' send.

What is this thing of beauty, engineered
With all man's genius, pistons, rivets, bolts,
Electrical impulses, flawless gears,
A nervous system sends a million volts...

Pressurised cabin, running water, food
That caters for all those religious needs...
'Oh, please, I'd like a vodka, but real cool,'
And all this at thirty thousand feet!

Strapped in and pampered, waiting eagerly
For treats, for drinks, for anything to make
Us happy and contented little souls,
But then the devil started to awake.

For him, the antichrist, this precious tube,
This scientific miracle of man,
This delicate assemblage made by few,
Is just a toy, to destroy with wanton hands.

Please shield us from all fears, since life is sweet,
By flying, do we not defy the gods?
From Prometheus, who stole the heat,
Put on your earphones, please, and gently nod.

Now sweaty Satan wakes to strike you down,
The beast, he comes in many different masks,
Sometimes he wears a beard and pious gown,
Yet underneath there lies a hungry shark.

While Allah weeps for every human soul
Whose flesh is mortified by cruel deeds

Performed by those who twist his holy words
To fit the hollow sterility of their creed.

Sometimes he hides behind the Torah's text
And claims to find within the sacred scroll
Some chinks in which to pour his poisoned dreck
While murder strides beneath the cleric's robes.

Likewise does Jesus Christ weep hard again
When his dear name is shrieked out like a curse,
And Irish men and women die in pubs
As ambulances race against the hearse.

So don't regurgitate your filthy lies
That God applauds your heinous hate-filled deeds.
God lives in every single flower that grows,
You are what chokes its life my friend... the weeds!

Filth, disease, and plague are in your hands,
War, fire, and famine will be your treats,
Anthrax is the perfume of their choice,
'God will bless it for us,' the madman shrieks.

The World Trade Center's elevators purr,
Racing to the peak their eager flesh,
Clasping in polystyrene cups their fuel,
Where it will sit undrunk upon a desk.

A silver bird reflects a shard of sun
That glints into her eye a mile away,
Of an office worker adding sums,
While idly glancing up into the day...

She sees it getting closer, closer still,
She thinks, 'My God, it's low, but this could be
One of those tourist planes forever filled
With eager eyes upon this panoply...'

'Oh, God, forgive me for every wicked thing,
Oh, darling, I love you till the end of time...'
And now the silver bird lifted its wing
While words of love were floating in the sky.

It was a quarter to nine, a bright blue morn,
We sentence you, poor ninety-two, to death,
Instead of walking in Los Angeles,
Prepare, my friend, to breathe your final breath.

It hit and what was once a thing of grace
Was then reduced to devastation, waste,
Black boiling oil, exploding outwards, flesh
Splattering the air, while lungs collapse.

It hit, we saw it, saw the sacrifice,
It seemed to dive into the tower's heart
And disappeared, just like a diver dives
Into the limpid water's yielding glass...

Just for a second when he reappears,
But now the bodies are shattered, split and melt,
Scattered, dropping, burnt and seared,
Flying bits of human, without seatbelts.

The building received a hell of a shock but hey!
Shook its head just once or twice, then grinned.
From that big slash that spread across its face
And belched dark poisoned smoke into the wind.

The city's eyes stared up in shocked alarm
For these two towers were like part of their lives,
Just as a mariner charts his boats by stars,
So do New Yorkers use them as their guide.

And now at nine-o-six, the second plane,
With sixty-five more victims sentenced too.

Did they see the towering inferno flames
Before their broken bones were turned to glue?

For thirty years or more the twins stood proud,
Glinting sharply in the morning light.
Sometimes they had their heads deep in the clouds,
But cheekily they winked at you at night.

Oh! Oh! Hang in there, bleeding, guts blown out,
Raging fires in your broken heart.
Hot oil trickling down your gentle throat,
Yet still standing like friends that will not part.

But then, oh then, you must forgive me please,
The punch I fear was stronger than we thought
And now I feel a buckling at my knees...
As far below two hundred firemen fought!

Now that its dearest twin had sadly died,
The other felt so lonely trembling there,
And even with its children trapped inside,
Crumbled. Slowly sinking in despair.

We saw two figures flying through the air;
Could ever we imagine such things to be?
We used to fly only in childish dreams;
They held each other's hands, the falling pair.

Poor Icarus fell to the bloody earth
When soaring far too close to the fiery sun.
His wings, so delicate, did slowly melt,
We heard the thud as bodies hit the mud.

The faces at the windows cried with rage,
And waved their pretty scarves and handkerchiefs;
'Help us, we're trapped inside a burning cage
And now the flames are nibbling at our feet!'

Oh pray, oh pray, for you good firemen
Who dashed into the dragon's fiery mouth
With helmets, gritted teeth and oxygen,
While up above them crashed the mighty house.

Sad widows clutch your smiling family snaps
And pour your tears onto your memories,
And you poor orphaned children who pine for dad:
Smell him in his wardrobe's history.

And mothers, fathers, brothers, sisters, friends,
Take each other's hands and make a ring,
To circumnavigate the entire globe
And then let's lift our heads and bravely sing!

REVENGE

Now Dubya gets upon his saddled horse,
Looks real ornery, squares his jaw and says,
'We'll smoke 'em out... You break our country's laws
And we'll getcha... Ain't nowhere you'll be safe!'

'Dead or alive!' the sheriff tells the world,
'We'll get them 'folks' who did this darned bad deed!'
Takes real big pauses 'fore he finds the words,
Like searching for a dime within the weeds.

Prefers to read the words of other men
Who craft the lines to make him look real smart,
Or else you'll squirm to watch him make some sense
And really hope he doesn't sound too daft.

Such sweet relief to hear the sounds of Blair...
Authoritative yet anxious, dipped in tears.
A quivering violin, it saws the air,
A master expressing the wounded world's despair.

'Snot to say that Dubya doesn't feel,
Though in their hundreds he snuffed out men's light,
In Texas prisons where the black man squeals,
Where few are reprieved the needle's vicious bite.

But now he's on the case; the country wakes;
It licks its wounds, is going for the kill.
America inspires an envious hate,
But now it's time for US to have our fill!

Burning anger scorches up the air,
We'll get you filthy bastards where you breed,

Just like some loathsome pestilence within its lair
You'll be exterminated with all your seed.

Just like a cancer builds its evil cells
By feeding on its very nourishing host,
We gotta zap it out, blast it to hell,
And turn those dirty bastards into ghosts.

America waits inside their cosy homes, Giant
fridges, TV sets the size of cars, Computers,
shop by Internet, mobile phones,
Cheap gasoline, burgers and singles bars.

The rich will sit in massive toy-filled flats
With views of Central Park or else Bel Air,
And movie stars will hold each other's hands,
And raise some dollars for the orphans' care.

But the poor, the simple, and the brave,
The families in Brooklyn, Bronx, and Queens,
The ancient ones who always are afraid
Lest illness strike and bring them to their knees.

Cause they forgot to keep the payments up,
Or took a gamble: 'Nah, I'm never ill...'
One day the wife complains she has a pain,
Oh God! The doctors feast on dollar bills!

But now, oh now, all is forgot today,
For now the nation stands together, says
'We are just one big family, USA,
And we'll fight together the American way!'

TV we watch with one collective eye,
In bars, hotels, in trailers or in the street,
As Dubya and Colin Powell display our might,
America flexes its muscles and bares its teeth.

'OK, scumbags, you wanna have a war?
OK, let's put our cards right on the deck,
I'll bet, tornadoes, Jaguars, VC tens;
I'll raise a few sea harriers and Tomahawks.

I'll add some guided missile cruisers too,
Some B-One bombers just to give it weight,
And nuclear submarines say 'Hi!' to you,
And then we'll see who's got the strongest hate!'

The relatives mourn the dead in shaded rooms,
Revenge, revenge, the wounded country cries;
Relishing the American eagle as it zooms
Into the darkening warlike eastern sky.

Revenge, revenge, pounds in the Yankee heart,
Black and white, Christian, Hindu, Jew,
And Muslim too; come on! They are a part
Of our great fabric; do not condemn them too.

Smite our enemies Lord, for Jesus's sake,
Onward Christian soldiers, marching onto war,
With the cross of Jesus, going on before...
We'll make them pay for what they did that day.

We'll make them pay, we will, Roko Camaj,
And you, Brad Sweeney, too, and dear wife Jules;
And John Ogonowski, pilot who safely flew
The thousands, oh, how much we owe to you!

For you, for all of you, young men so brave,
With metal hats in gold and shiny black;
The warriors who fight the tyrant flames,
For you, for all of you, who won't come back.

For you, Mike Quilty, fireman, just 42,
Three times a hero in the twenty years

You bravely gave, you selfless valiant few;
We will revenge you with our salty tears.

For with our tears we'll make so vast a lake
We'll drown them in their filthy hideaways
And when our bitter tears are dried up, gone,
We'll piss on you until your flesh decays.

For all of you, for all the secretaries,
Young women, innocent, full of female joy;
So many hundreds did we lose that day
Like flowers torn out the nourishing soil.

But now, oh now, oh yes, the man has come,
His name is whispered through the darkened streets,
And children being safely tucked in bed,
Into their small soft ears their ma will speak.

The time has come my little boys and girls,
No more the bad old ways, the man has come,
His silver tongue will soothe the savage beasts,
Our enemies will get down on their knees.

And on their knees they'll look at us and weep,
And say forgive us for our evil deeds,
And we'll say, you must forgive us too,
And then the dogs of war we'll put to sleep.

And that will be the day, oh, yes, oh yes.
The man has come to cleanse the house,
He'll open the windows to a bright new dawn,
And scour the basement of the rats and lice.

And into the house the sun will shine,
No more dark shadows and evil deeds,
The wind of change will blow them all away,
Away, away, please do it... Obama... Please!

The End.

POEM FOR THE NATION

So let us celebrate our victories abroad
We conquered foreign armies that would
Dare to lay their greasy paws on us
Our territories that like some far flung pearl
Round mother England's throat lay
In unprotected seas, so far away
We smacked the uncouth argy hand
And said let go your filthy fascist band
You dare to claim this spit of jutting rock
The last vestige of our almighty lands that
Once stretched over the world in British best
We must protect our nations far and wide
Our great and stalwart capitols of Stanley
Goose Green or Leigh on sea
Those teeming multitudes that lay in fear beneath the
    foreign yoke
Oppressed and forced by fascist brown faced thugs
To drive their cars on
Continental right than good old British left
Those men who died while landing on the beach
Those burnt alive in unprotected ships that like
A vat of oil did roast those tender limbs
Those drowning in the wild and icy foam
Will know that they die for Britain, not in vain
Those hundreds, thousands orphaned puking babies
Those widows howling in their lonely beds will yet take
    pride
To know that their brave boys, Mag Thatcher's kids were
    blown
Apart top stop worldwide oppression
Stop other dirty fascist foreign pigs claiming their spits

Of rock in far off distant climes
Good news our noble Thatcher, woman royal and doyen
   skirt will shriek
Our casualties are light today
No, not so many killed
Not many blinded
Chopped and slain
Our harriers did well
Too bad so many ships found speed burials
Still there will be more
There's orders in right now as Japan's shipyards sound
With clash of steel and chink of yen
So don't be sad your Mums and Dads
That gave your fruit to Thatcher's mighty gang
She'll not forget all that you gave
Those screams and smells of burning flesh of teenagers
That drown in icy flows will touch her heart
She'll feel, she's been a Mum as well
But most of all know this,
As yearly you do lay a flower by some unmarked sod
There'll always be a grave that is forever England!

DEDICATED TO THE ENGLAND TEAM

EUROPEAN CHAMPIONSHIPS SEMI-FINAL (26.06.1996)

Once more unto breach, dear friends, once more!
If Shakespeare were alive today, be sure
He would salute your skills in words so fine
That they would stir the dullest hearted soul
To pray for you this day, this special wed-nes-day.

But allow me, a humbler scribe to say to you,
That on the deep green fields of Wembley
Our hearts are beating faster for you boys
Until the whole of merry England pounds,
Its blood in one huge symphony.

The eyes of all shall fest with love on thee,
And whisper prayers for thy victory...
The village pub, in house, in hospital
In prison too the sentenced ones will smile
For you will swell our British pride again.

And oh how great that not a drop of blood
Is shed to stain the innocent and fruitful earth!
And that in craft and sportsmanship we fight,
Our weapons no more deadly than a bouncing ball,
So may this sport all gracious men unite.

DEATH ROW

I sit and wait and I sit and wait
I'm on death row baby and I have a date
When the bogyman straps me to my narrow bed
And my mama watches until they say I'm dead

No you ain't gonna hang and you aint gonna fry
You ain't gonna get the gas in your eyes
They got another day to make you die
Dey give you da needle for the paradise

The white man found yet another way
To send the Niggerman hopping to his muddy grave
And I'm really so grateful for all that he do
Cause the white man wants to make it easy for you.

So I sit and wait and I sit and wait,
Aint got no decent lawyer cause I got no cake
So I get what's provided by the good old state
Cause I never did get no educate.

Been sitting in my cell for a dozen or more years
While the papers go shuffling up and down the stairs
But my appeal seems to fall on deaf white ears
And my Ma is slowly running out of tears.

Now the death row's full of nasty old blacks,
Cause dey are the villains and they shoot you in the back
They peddle de power and we dress real cool,
Cause we didn't get taught nothing better at school

But when Uncle Sam needs us we're out there in the front,
Getting shot to pieces and we come home in a trunk

Give our lives gladly to keep the Yankee safe,
And the lucky ones who make it just stagnate.

Cause the school were rotten and the classes packed
Cause the taxpayers money don't go to the blacks
So when we went for a job, we didn't have the skills
But no mam, I didn't want to kill!

But the cops, they decided that I was the man
And there ain't no evidence except my brown tan
They picked me up cause I looked like the dude
But it don't really matter cause I'm getting what's due

So I fit the bill and I got a bad rep
In juvenile detention centres my skills were set
I went to the street and I peddle my dope

So I can pay for the doctor and give Ma hope
So farewell fellows and keep up the jive,
And yiz can all pretend I'm still alive,
But if you end up on the row just don't despair
Cause I'll be waitin for yiz up in the air!

THE ACTORS LIFE

What is this life, this dreary endless wait...
Will they use me or not? We'll let you know,
They liked you, the ever hopeful agent spake,
To be or not to be, the madman's role.

So what, so what... you chose this life, this pain,
To twiddle your thumbs, drive in the slow lane,
To chatter with some lost and forlorn dame,
And fantasise the parts you never played.

It passes well the time, the endless game,
I'd like to play Macbeth, I will one day,
And woo the audience to love me so,
And be impressed by my iambic flow.

And smile and hold each other's sweaty palms,
Be so amazed by dazzling vocal skills,
That I did practice daily on the rack,
Of unemployment, while idiots had their stomach filled.

But no, I don't need admiration's gaze,
Not just for that, am I a willing slave
But to give, to strive, to earn my pay,
By illuminating Shakespeare's page.

But then I worked and slaved on ancient texts,
And learn great speeches that I might perform,
In front of darkened mouths of theatres, tests,
To show you're fit to earn your grain of corn.

You might hold a spear or play the fool,
Be given vapid, stupid roles to learn

While waiting for the work that feeds your soul,
For that my heart with passion burns.

The audience with wide and hungry eyes.
Desire magic, sound and fury, fear,
Admire the great, the noble and the kings,
While your slim part stands quivering in the wings.

Before your entrance comes, the tannoy calls,
You step so swiftly down the endless stairs
And now you hear the cue, your footstep falls,
Onto the retinas of a thousand stares.

'What now endure... who is this dreary soul,
Another player yet to confuse our minds?
What is his purpose? Oh he is so drole,
Oh sometimes just how heavy weighs the time..

How long before the interval relieves
This tedious fellow from his dreary act?
Oh babble on you piece of worthless meat,
Meanwhile I think I'll take a quiet nap.

It's going well and better than I hoped,
The words are springing out and hitting home,
The audience though are restless, stupid drones,
When they should be alert to this great poem.

A coughing starts, erupting in the stalls,
Which like a forest fire throws it's sparks
On other coughers who had bravely welled
Their coughs in with a thumping heart.

But now the star has left hallowed stage,
They feel more free to discharge straining barks,
which stride like eager pups from owners mouths,
and now the sacred theatre's just a park.

117

But still the lonely small part player strives,
To organise his tiny well learned text,
Between the ripping sounds, his precious lines
Are layered with splutter, choke and stinking breath.

The lights go down, the curtain slowly falls,
And actors warble merrily their tales,
Oh how this line went well and that line palled,
And what a laugh was got while others failed.

And so the stars stared proud back at themselves,
Their makeup – enhanced features, they explored,
Oh yes my teeth are white as pearl seashells,
When lips are painted crimson, sharp and raw.

Oh how my slack cheeks now are sculptured rock
with shading to produce the thickened hair,
And eyebrows darkened, lined to bravely lock
My watery eyes into a hero's stare!

But me, the fill-in, plaster for the play,
Who tries to link the frail plot to make sense,
Up high with other splinters from the stage,
We humbly wait for act two to commence.

Some tea, a slow-dragged fag, a quick call home,
Makeup adjusted for the final scenes,
For those less occupied, and minds that roam,
Some scrabble eats the minutes till the tannoy screams.

'On stage, stand by' we swiftly leap downstairs,
The door is quietly opened on the deck,
The stage where Hamlet invites limpid stares,
Already tender hearted cheeks are wet.

Yes we are here to swell a scene or two,
A graveyard priest, a small oration there,

Not gabble, but make sense, the audience knew,
That we were just the spuds inside the stew.

So they can shut down their attention span
And give the brain a well deserved rest,
Consult the watch, programmes now a fan,
And dinner thoughts, yes, Sushi maybe best.

At last, at last, the ghastly show is done,
The punters bravely clap with sheer relief,
To get outside and stretch their pinioned bones,
Ah well, I saw the bloody thing, now... fish or beef!?

The actors string themselves together once again.
'Oh no, enough already, you've had your claps'
The star is bowing wanly, oh so 'drained',
For having bared his soul to all us chaps.

And now he bows down deeply, as if so moved,
By such a mild response from that shaggy lot,
11pm's last order or we will lose,
The table at the Ivy, we'll have to trot!

No more! We're getting out of here, lets fly,
Oh darling we're running a trifle late,
I thought the bugger would never die,
Of course I loved it, those bits when I was awake!

Another night is over for the prince,
Who washes off his makeup and the sweat,
Next door Gertrude and Ophelia whine,
Exchanging notes on how 'their' scene's a mess!

Of how Hamlet did this and how did that,
And he used them like two broken dolls,
Venting his raging passion while his spit,
Just landed on their faces like hot fat!

Never mind and sod it for theatres sake..
We have our weekly wage.. the parts a prize,
My boyfriend shags me faithfully twice a week,
No more than that in case his wife gets wise.

The play is over, put once more to bed,
The pieces reassembled every night,
Just like a jigsaw puzzle that you rend
And throw back in its box and out of sight.

But, this human, living jigsaw thrives,
And links it's pieces smartly like a clock,
You know the time it starts and when it dies,
Just wind it up once more, and hey, tic-toc!

It should get smoother running every night,
An actor lets the lines sink in his soul,
And pluck new cunning readings to delight
The audience, that often sit there like glum ghouls.

But no, not all, for some this is the treat,
A feast of Shakespeare, punning wit and verse,
To trick the ear as actors mark the beat,
They smartly giggle as those naughty couplets burst.

Oh, how jolly, clever, witty, smart and sage..
When Hamlet mocks the usurping king,
And drives the cunning villain in a rage,
As barbéd rhyming metres leave their sting..

And on and on, another night flies past,
The curtain drops, the stories rise and fall,
They clap, old stories told and actors laugh,
We wash the makeup off and mobiles call.

It's like.. it's like another day has passed,
Oh bliss, oh joy, I got through yet another,

My mind retained the clues that come so fast,
And now we have sweet freedom till the 'morrow.

But now, oh now, like dogs let off a leash,
So sweetly freedom floods into our veins,
We conquered yet again this ancient beast,
And now we play, yes, now the actors feast.

Will she meet me backstage now, I hope,
For now this shred of evening that is left,
Must fulfil my much depleted soul,
The first drink after work's always the best!

Oh darling, you were fab tonight, straight up.
A kiss, her cheek is autumn chilled smells sweet,
'You were so brill, and where we going to sup?'
'Joe Allen's good,' I didn't miss a beat.

'Really? I did feel better, yes, tonight.
The lines they seemed to snap out of my mouth,
Like arrows, swift and piercing, straight in flight,
Each night is different of that I have no doubt.

'Oh yaa! It's different, that's for sure, OK'
'But tell me darling was I at my best?'
'Of course, that's what I mean, you caught the play,
Oh god, I'm dying for some chicken breast!'

So down the nimble stairs we trot all keen,
Observe the posters pinned like flags of state,
That advertise the plays that died last week,
Table for two, yes, smoking if that's ok.

'But oh, your fellow actors are out of joint,
As if they're curling slightly at the edge,
Like boredom starts to seep in and it stales,
Their once enthusiastic thespians' breath.

A carafe of your best, house wine, I mean,
A Caesar salad and that great bean soup,
A burger, medium rare and that's for me,
The soups as thick as tar and makes you poop!

'For madam, breast of chicken and French fries,
There's Michael Gambon, an actor now well sought
He's doing the L.A bit I see these days
It's better than earning twopence at the Court!

Oh isn't that the critic Nick de Jong?
He's grinning now just like he's skinned a cat,
He's so appealing when his claws are out,
And tears the throat out of some turgid crap.

There's Alec Macowan, isn't he looking well?
His profile seems to slice the very air,
And if his words were fruit, they'd be so sweet,
Of all the actors, I think he was most rare.

The wine is quaffed and hungry mouths devour,
While eyes explore the tables eager guests,
Few actors now, more musicals inspire
The twirling dancers to Joe Allen's nest.

We pay, and snake between the tables roar,
And smile at one, at others flick a wave,
The night ensnares us in its carbon shawl,
A taxi hailed and through the night we sail.

But yet the nights not over, still the blood,
Is heated by the stages fierce demands,
But slowly, slowly does the soul give up,
Those precious pearls of freedom that it won.

And now the memory of that victory fades,
As daily life and matters drive away,

The glorious conquest of your escapade,
And makes us smell the sourness of the day.

We wake, I fill the kettle, light the stove,
Pour green tea in the strainer, organic too,
I cut two slices from a dark brown loaf,
And grill it blackly while the kettle boos.

There was a bakery, end of Berwick street,
Whose bread was crunchy and dark hued,
Next door a deli sliced smoked salmon, neat,
And pickled cucumbers were munchy Jews

And down the market stalls, in summers heat,
I'd buy the softest avocado pears,
And button mushrooms, tender as soft teats,
Fat red tomatoes, chicory, picked with care.

Oh how I loved that coloured fruit-filled stroll,
Amongst the slush of battered spinach leaves,
Crushed grapes that fallen from the stalls,
Lay split, and slithery, spewing out their seed.

My shopping bag was full, the red bus leaps,
Some pounds still stuffed in wallets soft caress,
How lovely to get wages every week,
The toast is crisp and salmon drapes it's breast.

A tray is carried to the basement room,
'How sweet you are' the sleepy magpie sings,
Oh lovely, gurgle, bite, she lifts the gloom,
From the grey-sky'd, heavy morning London scene.

She goes, she was my schooner of the night,
That sailed me through my darkness and despair,
I clung to my heaving craft with all my might,
And safely reached the shores with loving care.

There's something special in the honey'd sleep,
Betwixt a lover and his sweetest miss,
Incomparable and endless bliss,
But then in youth, too often passion shrieks.

But as the heart grows wiser, knowledge soars,
And renders flesh and spirit in one grip,
For lust, when passing leaves a deadly bore,
Since true loves pleasures are just infinite.

Two pulsing bodies sweetly move as one,
An awesome awareness of the joy of this,
Makes love, the only eventual outcome,
Where you'll find heaven, even in a kiss.

But now the flat is cold, and dull, remote,
Absent of the glow that gave it warmth,
Slouch in a bath and feed the mewing cat,
And scuttle down the road like a timid rat.

The hours are on your side but only just,
Until the large hand slowly slides past twelve,
And then you start to watch the minutes pass,
And thus begins the slow descent to hell.

A mind in hell is not a pleasant place,
A little demon robs you of peace and calm,
You even dream of running off the stage
To sanctuary, comfort and soothing balm.

But that's the usual angst before the stage,
Expectation with a twitch of fear,
But in the dressing room with all your mates,
Their lively chatter makes the world more clear.

Their energy and strength inspires yours,
Their love is like a life-line that you seize,

And you give them, your loves returned,
Although you feel your courage in your knees.

But soon this will be over and our group,
That was so close and intimate today,
Living for each other's words to hook
Our own words to and make the play.

We smell each other's breath and feel the sweat,
Our very lives depend upon each soul,
And so in such a strong and keen embrace,
We hold each other up, and that's our role.

Our role on stage and then again in life,
Don't be a thief and steal his precious laugh,
Because the actors skill is like a light,
That will expose a grubby pirates craft.

But be all generous and learn from all,
Respect their heartfelt talents, conflicts, end!
You will shine in their reflected glow,
And let your final curtain fall, with friends!

NO! OLD MAN

Poor man, he senses he's growing old
His raging storms of youth are just
A fading memory when strong and bold,
When snatching flowers by the roots
And crushing strawberries between your teeth
And wearing mohair, hand tailored suits

And dancing the perfumed night away,
Your hair was thick in twisted curls
Your muscles shimmered like an ocean spray,
You spun out words like string for pearls
And placed them gently in her ears
And then you claimed your special girl

Then, you thrashed and heaved and scooped
The loving flesh between your thighs
Between your hands, your mouth, oh how you wooed
On your night long trips to paradise.
Wet kisses danced between your lips
Like glistening shoals of silver fish

So the memories make their ghostly dance
Across your aging lovers eyes.
How they sweetly taunt and prance
As you stare out at threatening skies,
As you lay squeezing the last few drops
From the shrivelled fruit of your distant lives.

Don't moan, Oh I can't shower
The earth with my once precious dew
Oh I can't summon lightning bolts of power

To rent the mighty oak on cue,
Oh I can't cause her knees to quake
And mighty rivers to churn and stew.

But think old man, those heavy years
That pile upon your aching bones,
Are not a cause for choking tears
Painful regrets and dying groans
Look how the death of each new day
Is blazoned bright in stark sunsets
The heavens celebrate in brilliant cascades
As the golden sun dips in the fiery west

So what, no longer, bold young rake
With pounding, spitting, shrieking nights
Unfaithfulness and scattered babes
New brides with firm young flesh to taste
And then discarded, broken, shamed
While you hunt new game like a bird of prey

But think old man, no need to pine
Your once firm bride is now your friend
Supporting your old carcass till the end of time
As you do her, as you laugh and cry
Cause now you change cheap lust for love,
She becomes your mother with a sweetened sigh.

And she, in all the years you are entwined
Becomes your little sparking girl,
That you with such gentle caring eyes
Watch over your prodigy.
Sometimes a loving sister she will be,
Nursing your pains, soothing your woes
And you a playful brother will tease
And make her giggle from head to toe.

So think old man what you possess
Open wide those huge sad eyes of yours

As age begins its slow caress
It opens may other doors
For now you have a mother, sister, daughter, friend
And she a father, brother, son and mate

Who would exchange such a wealth of love
For the conflicts of passion, oft ridden with hate.
Your ages bequeaths you so much wealth,
Your souls, ten fathoms deep with love
No! Not old, old man on bended knees
But young, flying on the wings of a dove.

WIMBLEDON

He throws the ball
High in the air
His arm is raised
Now don't despair
His racket's gripped
Makes a tight fist
Gotta win this point
Just one serve left

And whack, he whacks it
Oh so hard
A meteor tears
Through the sweaty air
And is it in or is it out?
The crowd just gasps
The girlfriend pouts
And grips her hair
Oh! Oh! Don't despair.

She's staring at him
Like for her
He is the only thing
Worth living for.
Her heart is pounding,
Pounding fast
Oh how much longer
Can this game last?
'Cause every game
He plays, she's there
And every time
He hits the ball

It's like her heart
That feels the thump,
It's like her heart
That beats as fast
As the balls go
Spinning past

And mama, mama's
Watching too
This valiant guy
Came from her womb
Those rippling muscles
Are her flesh
He was a puppy
In her nest
And now, and now,
He's mighty sleek
Tears up the court
Like a raging beast
She's watching every
Move he makes
Watching when
He lifts his cap
Watching when
He wipes his brow
Watching when
He slugs a drink
Watching, watching,
Mama proud
So is it in
Or is it out?
The electronic eye,
will sort it,
Yes sort it out.

And yes, it's in!
A tiny sliver

Just covers the line
The opponent quivers.
It's just a shadow,
A belly's curve
But enough to make
The damn point mine!
The girlfriend shivers

Oh God another set
To play, oh why
Won't this man go away?
But he won't
He won't go away
He wants to break you
So make his day
Ok pal, it's time to play.
The crowd is hushed
The sun beats down
They gasp or shout
Or wince or frown,
Or giggle and gape
Some play the clown
Just a typical
English crowd

They can't believe
How long it lasts
The ladies like
The sinewy thighs
They like these
Superhuman guys.
They like their arses
When they bend
When they crouch down
To start the set
Their white shorts, white
As snow and crisp

Their sculptured arms
Their rock hard tits
And most of all
Their guts, the way
They stand before
The massive throng
Whilst the punters urge
Their favourite on

They stand there proud
And twirl their rackets
Waiting for the meteor strike
And show no fear
Eyes laser-like
From where the ball
Will spit at you
A great white glob
Spat through the air

How handsome men are
When they fight
How fierce like animals
When they show their might
The ladies keep these thoughts
Real quiet
And utter sweet and melting sighs
As their lust filled eyes
Just graze their thighs

Their boyfriends wish
They'd some of it
The boyfriends wish
They had their balls
The boyfriends wish
Their girlfriend's eyes
Adored them so much
As these superguys

OK, it's two sets each
It evened out
The Swiss guy looks
A little wan
Like his candle's gonna
Be snuffed out
Yet he's the dude
Real cool, real calm

Thick hair tied with
A cummerbund
His sponsor's logo
On his chest
Why he don't look
Like he even sweats
He's waiting for
The Yank to serve

Fingertips strum
The racket's strings
He knows that his
Opponent serves
Like the ball
Had sweptback wings
Like a shot
From a cannon's mouth

It's faster than
A speeding Jag
Swifter than
A plunging bird
Ready to pierce
It's silvery prey
As it glides innocent
In the foaming spray

The Yank, he tests
The balls each time

Poppity poppity poppity pop
He pockets one
The other's ok
He does the same thing
Like a rhyme
Like a ritual
He must obey

Bouncing the ball
Yes, just three times
Is he sending a message
To the Gods of the game
Whose names are mounted
Now up high
The greats, whose sweat
Has drenched the courts
Whose steel sprung thighs
Had raced and leapt,
Scissorr'd over the turf
Hands outstretched
Heart pounding, veins bulging,
Lungs aflame
Oh yes, the masters
Of the game.

Their legends live
Now for all time
On the pantheon
They are enshrined
But now their shadow
Selves remain
Dressed in suits,
Hair turned to grey

A dishy number
By their side
To give these champs

A little pride,
But as she sits,
Her skirt rides high.
But when they enter
The viewing stands
The crowd bursts into
Warm applause
Oh, is this not,
The sweetest sound
The loveliest music
The ex champ hears
Like the fluttering of
Angel's wings
Wafting the odour
Of ancient games
Into the nostrils
Of these ex-kings

Susurrating through
The hot June air
Now, the old champs
Stare right down
Seeing their young selves
On the green
Remembering what it was like
To feel ten thousand eyes
Demand a kill

Watching you dance,
Leap, twist and turn
That impossible ball
You returned
Watching the muscles
Writhe in their skin
Watching your grace,
Your poise, your spin
But now another

Takes your place
Another's standing
In your shoes
Another hand will
Smash an ace
Another one
Will win or lose

It soars, it swoops,
It hits the square
So fast it scorches
Up the air.
He can't return it,
He's not that fast
That's beyond just
Any man to grasp

That's beyond what
Mortal man can do
Outside of what
Is possible
40 love, another hit,
Oh God he wants to
Bloody spit
Bloody aces
Make him sick

Just look into his eyes
And see, the fires
Beginning to subside
4 hours hey! It's
Just too much
Hit and smash,
And whack and crack
The sun now gets
Into the act.
Zoom! Keblam!

Drop shot! Volley!
Poor girlfriend slowly
Turns to jelly

Oh there's a royal
Looking so smart
And there's a nebbish
Woody Allen,
Russell Crowe is looking mild
All actors are impressed
By heroes tearing up
The turf, the ring
Rough waters, land
Just anything
Since actors only make-believe
The stand-in does
The real hard stuff,
To make it look
The actor's tuff
No stand-in here
For these two dudes
Now almost half the
Weight they seemed
Before they stepped,
Onto the green
But still they fight,
They hit, they play
The ball is just

A stain across
Your retina, it goes so fast
Just how much linger
Can it last?
Just now, they're
Eating up their flesh
Just now they're
Drinking their own blood

Just now they're
Feeding on reserves
Just now their
Stomach's turned to mud
But still, but still
But still, but still
They'll play until,
Their flesh drops off

Until their muscles
Turn to glue
Until their limbs
Are held by threads
Zoom! Keblam!
Drop shot! Volley!
The girlfriends face is
Turned to putty

Her eyes stare blindly
Stabbed with pain,
No longer is this
A tennis match
This is a tryst
Whose end is death
Unless just one of them
Succumbs or else his heart,
Bursts in his chest.

They could play
For evermore
As if it was
Some punishment
Just like narcissus
Poor vain thing
Turned to a flower
By a stream

Or like Prometheus
Feeding his flesh
Every night, for evermore
His poor tired liver
Is shredded raw.
So don't provoke the jealous god
But know your place
You're just poor sods

Or else you'll feed
The Gods your gore
So these two
Superhuman men
Be careful lest
You're turned into
Just two small stinking
Sweaty pools

But now the Yank
Has missed the ball
He missed the one,
The important one,
The one that sends him,
To Kingdom Come
The one upon
Which text is writ....

'He who lets
This ball go past
His reputation
Will not last
He who fails
To send me back
Will be forever
On the rack

Remain forever
In the plains

Where also-rans
Bide out their time
He who lacks
The final surge
Will forever
In his mind

Play the game
Time after time
'If only I'd done
This or that'
His mind will be
A nest of rats
Yes, forever
On the rack

Thank God it's over
Over now,
The happy crowd
The simple folk
Who seldom tear
Themselves apart
To entertain folks
With their art

Who never sweat
And break their hearts
To go that extra mile
Or even die
That we may watch
TV and send email
And make the tea.

The crowd applauds
The winner, loser too
Who looks forlorn
As if the world

Has tossed him out
Into deep space nine
The Swiss one smiles
And walks the court

He's waving to the
Cheering throngs
Who now can stand,
Their flattened arses
Slightly numb
But now how strange
He dons a coat,

Holds the cup up
To his lips,
It's gold and gleaming
And his kiss
Is like a kiss
For all of us
But wait, what is that
On his wrist?
That's on his wrist,
what's that?

Some magic bracelet,
Shining bright
Some talisman
Like Arthur's sword
Rending immortality
To those who wear it?
Yes, it's a Rolex
Glittering steel

Did our hero,
Even at this time
Where life and earth
Almost collide

And with the hope
Of millions on his head
His wife and baby
Nearly bursting through

In years to come
She'll tell the child
When daddy triumphed
I felt you writhe
Felt you moving
In my womb
Like you my sweet
Were cheering him
But yet the Swiss man
At the end
When half the world
Stood up and yelled
When even the Gods
Themselves were quelled
Remembered to put
His Rolex on
For now the Gods
Are sponsors
Never offend
And if they say
'Please, let your cuff
Slip down your arm
So the world may see
The gifts that Heaven brings
Our mighty Rolex, glittering

So all is past
And home they go
Old champions comment
For the TV screen
Pontificate
and make shrewd chat

Illuminate our
Weary minds
To tell us what
We missed or failed

To see with their
Professional artistry
And so farewell
Dear Wimbledon,
And to you all
Sampras, Becker,
Borg, Agassi,
Navratilova, gorgeous Gussie

Billy Jean King and Steffi Graf
McEnroe and Nastase
Roger Federer Andy Roddick
And know that
Every ace you played,
Every impossible return
Will be a star
In that great mighty urn
of heaven.
So farewell to you all.

KEAN

Oh dearest Edmund Kean, your light shines far
Across the centuries' turbulent years
Like stars whose illumination glows still fresh
Although its body quietly lays at rest.
So you in dust in some forgotten tomb,
Neglected, broken, no stone marks the place,
Still stand in mankind's eye, brightest by far,
Commanding centre stage, triumphant star.

Almost two centuries have spread their seeds
Of conflict, strife and witnessed endless seas of blood,
And soulless men have poisoned precious streams
And politicians preach war makes us free
And yet the basic truth the poet sees,
Whose words do teach the heart's true mysteries,
And actors, now the poet's messengers
Reveal like sacrificial offerings

Their nerves and sinews, rip apart their chest,
Their palpitating heart gives words a beat,
a tongue of flame gives text the magic breath
Which pours into the printed words the heat.
So Kean, the small in stature, giant in heart,
With sweat he oiled the boards of Drury Lane,
Shylock was his first choice, pathetic Jew,
A spat-upon, whose vengeance was to hew

A pound of choicest flesh from Christian breast
Kean's chance, his first, his opportunity
To plunge into the city's cultural sea;
He made the biggest splash, he passed his test.

His waves drowned out his gaping fellow thesps
Whose screeches as they gasped were bitter, harsh
'Tis just a passing phase, dear, cannot last',
They dearly hoped and fervently did pray...
For he had set a standard far too high,
And now their feeble efforts would look pale
To one who's seen the sun with naked eye
And so a meteor flew into our sky...
Yes, Kean the great had waited far too long,
His toil, a preparation for this time,
The endless struggle starving for his art
Had made his mind and body a sharpened knife.

And like his Richard III, his great success,
He'd hew his way into the public's breast.
The daily torment of his early years
When he would choke his memory with words,
That must that night be played in blood and tears
Before the mind digested each new part,
Was now, thank God, a torment of the past
Yet this had turned his vocal chords to strings...

Upon whose chords he'd play a symphony,
The miles of highway that his legs had trod
With Howard Kean, his infant, on his back
Had made his legs like Atlas-bearing oaks,
And there he stood as if rooted to the stage
As if the very planks had born this prodigy.
The ancient wood delighted with his steps
As if they felt a kindred sympathy,
At last, they thought, a new Prometheus.

He'd drunk the cup of pain right to the dregs
and then licked up the scummy residue
While others still sucked the milk of mother's breast
Young Ed did thread the maze of London's streets,
Learning, as one must, the night from day

He saw that rich and poor divide the sweets
One stuffs so much until their gorged throat heaves,
the other pounces on what the rich do leave.

The one is fat and bloated, pale and wan,
The other lean and bony, rough and hard,
The one is sickly happy, never pleased,
The other finds sheer bliss in bread and lard,
So Edmund's eyes and ears devoured the sights
Behind the scene, while watching endlessly
The tumult and the traffic of the stage
While still a boy when everything does taste
With fiery intensity of youth,
Unspoiled, unsullied by indulgences' glut,
His agile mind fed deep upon the words
Watching great actors create life from dust.
As did the ancients that one day in Prague
Create a human from the river's bed,
so do great actors bring to vivid life
the words that slumber in unopened texts.

The words that centuries ago were forged
And now enshrouded in archaic fog
Too laboursome to read, to trace the thoughts
That bred these titans, these dramatic gods.
The heroes of the stage must be released
Must be unchained from their imprisoned page
Where like dumb prisoners they sadly lay
Waiting for the one to snap those chains.

And so the actor loans his voice and soul
His heart and lungs and too his hands and face,
His eye, his lip, his tongue and flowing breath
And yes he brings back Hamlet from cold death,
Yes, Othello, and Iago too,
Richard the Third with hump struts once again
Awoken from his ancient filthy tomb

To demonstrate the sweetness of vile sin.
And now the heart of Romeo pumps fresh,
Filling the eyes of Juliet with tears,
So like an ancient river bed run dry,
The actor brings fresh torrents from the sky.
Just like those fabled rainmakers in drought
With magic deeply learned made heaven weep
So actors swallowing those words so dry
Feed them gently with their living ink.

And now we laugh, we tremble, and we cry
As poor Hamlet sucks his final breath,
Oh how we bite our lip and sadly sigh,
As Desdemona faces cruel death.
Oh yes, some academics love to advise,
'To read it in my home, I much prefer,
Turning the pages, making visions rise,
Not suffering dreadful actor's mangling verse!'

But then there is a different alchemy
As when one thousand faces sit and stare
Feeding each other's mutual sympathy,
Becoming brothers and sisters in despair.
As Macbeth slays the gentle Scottish king
And then plots Banquo's most appalling death
As Cleopatra feels the serpent's sting
A thousand heaving bosoms hold their breath

An actor feeds a multitude at once,
The reader feeds his solitary self,
Great comfort can be said to read alone,
And make the theatre of the mind your own.
And yet no greater pleasure can be had
Then have to sit in sweaty intimacy
with heaving bodies and their foul breath
While some poor coughing idiot mars the text!
Just when the actor reaches ecstasy,

his form, his skill, his judgement for the hit,
prepared the way to lift the words to heights
some bleeding cougher then puts out the lights!
Splitting, choking, ripping away the veil,
The magic that the actor painfully weaves
To transport us to other magic worlds
Alas, we crash into reality!

For brief few moments we were in Padua,
Or in the idyllic perfumed forest glades,
Flying with Oberon over the violet banks
While lovers slumber in the evening shade.
But now, alas, we're back with stinking mouths,
The rank effusion of their rotting guts,
The smell of tallow candles sputtering out
And idiots whose attention span is slight...

And shift and fidget when their lowly brains
Cannot interpret higher sentiments,
But wait until the text once more descends
To levels where their idiocy comprehends
And yet, and yet, in spite of all this grief
That would cause a mighty warrior to blanch,
Once the actor bravely takes on this brief
We watch as slowly he entraps our hearts.

And now the thousand shifting moving souls
Are strangely still, the concentration caught,
No longer can we smell the rancid flesh
For we are sitting in a world apart.
Only the great ones can turn lead to gold,
To change an overheated heaving pit
Into a temple where the priest unfolds,
The agony of mankind's wretchedness.

Its suffering martyrs on the cross of love
Whereby the young do die for passions lust,

Repressed by elders jealous grasping claws
Who would deny what they themselves had lost.
Or else describes the hero's selfless feats
When Rome was ruler of the ancient world
And share with brave Marc Anthony his grief
As he mourned Caesar's bleeding gaping wounds.
Some one of us has had a life denied,
Perhaps an early dream lay unfulfilled

Conjured as children when our hopes were bold
But then as adults fear turned courage cold.
So at the theatre we escape and join
Our heroes and our suffering heroines
And snatch a little spark of courage back
By imagining that we are them!

And only this can great actors achieve,
To seize us by our hearts and minds and souls
Impressing us by their passion's industry
To make the coward think that he is bold.
So Kean was shaped and forged on England's stage
For many years this meteor lit the skies
Each town was one more struggle as he raged
Against humiliation, sneers and lies.

Mocked, reviled, condemned to play the clown,
So he excelled in every task he takes
Became a brilliant harlequin, renown,
For spinning through the air with perfect grace.
His size they jeered, 'tis not of heroes made,
Too short, by far, we seek great Kemble's grace,
Tragedians are not small, they are kingsize,
Sorry old boy, slap on your clown's red face.

But genius grows just like the precious pearl,
What, though he danced and tumbled like a clown,
Such crafts he used to underpin his skill,

To give him techniques beyond the actor's drill
Who nothing knew except to learn by rote,
Who seldom forced their limbs to master crafts,
That felt too lowly for their hallowed 'art'
And so predictably they played their parts.

So unaware that skills of mime or dance
Could add to their performance much grace
Since nothing learned upon this wondrous earth
Will in a mind that's "Kean" just go to waste.
So Kean was shaped by circumstance to be,
The ruling King of Shakespeare's tragedy
And so his suffering and his bitter woe
Gave brilliant insights to his greatest roles.

His torments, as for pittances, he slaved,
Grew in his bank of passion, interest paid,
And when to Drury Lane was sudden called
He drew from his vast wealth to feed his art,
And Shylock for his premiere stunned the stalls
For Kean was just a millionaire at heart.
The actors were alarmed before they mocked,
When Kean appeared in wig as black as jet,

Since Jews as villains must wear always red,
The simple customs of the pliant slave,
Who follows others dumbly as the night the day
But this man breaks old customs, makes his own,
Let others blandly chew on sucked out bones.
Kean leads, his meteor's fiery tail will scorch,
The others who attempt to dog his steps,
Since genius walks alone, his pride... his crest!

No gold, nor riches can ever replace,
The richness in the mind of the human race,
Since money only feeds the swollen gut
Imagination's wealth surpasses that.

A voice, a gesture in pursuit of truth
Cannot be much improved by fortune's bribe,
Nor dare a poet attempt to inspire the muse
By dangling baubles in her pretty eyes.

Only with an eye that's witnessed pain,
That all who sweat and slave must needs endure,
Who feels and shares the world vicissitudes,
Can make his art the medicine to cure.
Can then bring to the stage a thousand parts,
The way a master painter celebrates
The world in luscious brilliant paint
So too, the actor's palette is his heart.

BIG GAME FISHING

The great jaws open, a crushing bite,
the hook goes in – it's piercing sharp,
but, oh, a shock, what fish is this,
that drives its spike right through my mouth?
What prey is this that stabs my jaw,
and won't let go, some vicious tooth?
A broken rib or shattered spine?
I can't escape the nasty claw that's ripped into my lips and
    mouth,
can't shake it free and when I pull,
it breaks my teeth and tears my jaw,
rips into my gullet, shreds
my tongue, the agony is fierce!

"Hey Joe, we gotta big one hey!
just look at the sonofabitch, it's huge!
and wow, those fuckin fins are wide.
hey it's a goddam bloody beaut!"

His ample guts flop over his belt
His stumpy legs shoot from his shorts
He puffs and pants, his fat neck sweats,
Veins are bulging, eyes, excited big,
Grabs a beer from out the cooler
It dribbles over his thin red lips.
The rod is tightly gripped, it bends,
The sailfin fish is fighting hard,
fighting for life, with all its might,
grinding its teeth against the hook,
knowing somehow that a crack appears,
a rent in the precious blue of life,
a crack where only grim death sneers

"Hey you motherfucker, hey you beast,
I'll getcha, shit! It's got some strength,
wanna take the rod, my hands are chafed,
hey wanna take the rod, it's got some pace!
reel it in, real slow...don't snap
it's slowing down, it's tiring, shit!
Ha! ha sweetheart, we'll get you yet"

Confusion, where once I swiftly sped
sliced the foam, divided the waves
pierced the green and unguent gloom,
so easily chased the bass, stingray
the silver barracuda fish, that hang
in the sea like shiny blades,
the multi-coloured parrot fish,
could even crush the stony crab,
But now!
Upon the breast of the heaving brine
that was my mother, my terrain,
where I, yes ever, shaped like a wave,
rode the endless sun-licked sea,
felt the endless currents deep,
the endless shake of mothers embrace.
What is this monstrous beast, I eye,
catching a glimpse, 'tween sea and sky.
See this grinning lump of meat -
a gross misshapen cackling beast,
what is this malformed creature, fish or fowl?
No wings, or claws, or scaly sides,
but yet has stabbed me, thrust a hole,
slashed me with a piercing bite!

"Gaddam! we're nearly there, yahoo!
It's tiring, it's tiring, rein her in!
Spool in slowly bit by bit,
look at those fuckin sailfins wow!
Oh yeah, oh she is a beaut alright.

And this will make our great 'grand slam!'
Wow! our ninth! yahoo! top shit!

How he grins, this one proud man,
Proud of the lives, he gamely snuffed,
Robbed from the belly of the sea,
Torn from out the proud sea's womb,
Stabbed and thrust, and pierced and cut,
In steel capped boats with stinking plumes,
As petrol stains the velvet green,
And stopped the lives, oh so abrupt.
For what? so he can show the world,
He is a man.
It's what men do.
To demonstrate to all the world,
The skill in killing defenceless beasts
It's fun!
In cutting short a creature's life
Or are they just large things that float,
And give you all a day of fun,
With bored sloppy wives who cheer
And as they writhe and twist and leap and turn,
Desperate, trying to escape,
She captures it on her video cam.

Weakening, too weak now to resist,
my blood is pouring, pouring out,
but still, I have my bite, my bite,
if only I could bite the head,
from off this stinking cackling beast,
but now a blow has stunned me hard,
rough arms drag me from the world,
I feel so heavy, so ill at ease,
I'm panting hard for every breath,

'Hey get your camera, over here
big bastard, you gave us quite a fight!'

I feel the life begin to leak
oh let me, let me back to die,
oh let me, slowly, slowly sink

'You got it! great, now I'm the best,
the world's best, no-one can dispute!'

Oh let me back into the green,
into the green and tumbling sea,
yes let me go, even your stink,
is just beyond, just anything,
that I have nosed within the deep!
The beasts are shouting, cheering, yelping, shriek!
Is this mankind of which I've heard,
but never ever before seen?
'Gotta full house now, bring out the beer!
yahoo, yaha! ya got the pic?
I'm the world's greatest fisherman! shit!'
Oh let me slowly slowly sink
into the deep, into the blessed, blessed deep.

ISRAEL.

SEPTEMBER 1985.

The sea in Israel is soft and blue
Azure, or topaz, aquamarine
The waves roll in their velvet tongues
Lick you, roll you over, you dry in the sun

The voices whisper on the sands
The babble of the broken race
That's put together back all wrong
All the pieces in a different place

Here a Russian, here a Czech
Here Romanian, Serbian, Pole,
French or German, Dutch or Greek
They all play tennis on the beach

They came in boats, by plane, by road
To the sanctuary of the heart
To where the blood can pump again
No scattered, bleeding, torn apart

They came by night, morn, afternoon, dusk
Every vehicle that moved... went.
Crammed full, don't forget her doll
The pain behind faded real slow

The dark primitive Aryan hordes
Struck, killed, or just snubbed sometimes
No entrance here, no work, no rights, no home.
They packed their suitcase with string.

We don't need more hints, we're on our way
Wretched lands we gave our due
We paid the tax, cured a few of you
Left some culture, and a revolution too!

The sea pointed the way
The waves carried us away
The boats drifted on the tides of history
No navigator that day

The heart was calling us in
The blood raced to the pump
Wanted to flow with its own
United at last in the soul

We heard the call one morn
Scratching for food the barren earth
Our permitted allotment for ones
That murdered God's only son

We saw a blood red dawn
Behind the chimney pots
We heard voices in the wind
The fires blazed in a rush

We sat and eyes opened wide
The heart pumps quicker too
We heard some went to the desert
Where the sun shone even on Jews

The smell of freedom was strong
You awoke with its tang
Throw things in a case
How the heart sang

Movements were spreading, cracks in the earth
Shoots in cement, freedom at last

Lips moving faster, Zion is here
There is a place not stamped yet, fear!

The sea caresses soothes and strokes
All on the beach the family at last
Grandma, Mum, Dad and the Kids
One gigantic family of yids

Yids from every different village and town
Street and country, state and shtetl
Yids from Vienna with silken gowns
Yids from Kiev, Bialystok, Odessa.

Yids from the revolution torn
In 1905 that failed, still born
Yids from the pogroms in the night
The Cossacks cruel sword catches the light

The blade slashes down, off comes a hand
A nose, an eye, slash again
An arm, an ear, a thigh
Don't anger the gentile beast... fly!
Horses in the night, tanks in the night
Shouts in the night, screams in the night
Nightmares in the night, dying in the night
Parting in the night... it was all night

When was the night for sleeping
When was the night for loving
When was the night for dreaming
There were some good times... not all bad!

They didn't always come, years passed
We built schools, temples, theatres too
Had kosher cafes in Berlin, really?
Yes, the life was normal, was true
Built offices, factories, whadya mean? Banks!

Oiled the finances on the market place
Had barmitzvahs... 'cost a fortune!'
Had curtains in silk and hems in lace.

Theres a place where the sun shines
The sea is pure silk and lazy pace
It's a desert, nobody hates you
Or wants to spit in your face
Whatya mean? We're happy in Dusseldorf
Aum Rhine... we have a nice business
Keep our noses clean, and surgeons take
The curve out to give us that gentle sheen

How come the hooked nose
Stops the sand getting in
Look at the camels too
The Arabs have them and the Hebrews

We don't need the hook, our badge
We speak high deutsche, eat crab
Drink fine wine, read Goethe
Adolph who? Sorry, we're off to the opera

The sea rolls in and washes us away
Lifts us up and down and cleans
The sand makes a bed beneath our feet
And the stars will come out each night

The families gather on the eve of Shabbat
Old ladies and men gabble in chewed up tongues
Language ripped apart and then sewn up
Like an old coat made from borrowed cuts

In the seas early morn, like gulls on the wave
They gather, the last flock to re-unite
In their broken words they make a coat

Of multi colours that won't be rent!

They came from Russia, from pogroms
Leaving their ears or their hands or feet
We can pick one up in Tel Aviv
Maybe in Ben Yehuda Street

The sky is every day a perfect shade
From puce to ivory, sometimes deep dyed
On Shabbat they pour out on the beach
Or pray to God in Torah-speak.

There was a town called Plonsk
Which was as ugly as its name
One day a pamphlet was read
Don't waste your lives away
Why crawl and hug the wall
Why whisper while you pray
Just in case you anger them
That pray to god in other ways

Why simper in darkened shtetl rooms
Fear the clattering through the streets
Have papers, licenses, obey bent laws
Listen to the bastards while smelling their stink.

One day some pamphlets came to Plonsk
A young boy... on his way to school
Clutched the words that shook and stunned
Ate them and flew to the sun

Across the steppes the Clarion call
The sound reverberated across the earth
Return to Zion, throw down the curse
Your half-dead lives in the nether world

In Bucharest they fled, across the fields
Swam in the dark protection of the night

Lines of ants, rivers of flesh and blood
Clutching their possession... and the Talmud.

They can now put into practice 'the word'
Not just pray it, but dig it in the earth
Not mourn it, worship and love it now
And drink the vine of Israel

Now no-one can blame the bloody yid
For all the trouble in their lands
From Russia, Poland and Deutschland
Another scape-goat must be found

We didn't poison wells in Nuremburg
We didn't eat children in Lincoln town,
We didn't drink blood in Kiev
Find other outlets for your lazy heads

You slaughtered me in York, England
You burned me in Madrid
You hung me in Nuremburg
You butchered me in Kiev

You gassed me in Treblinka now
With german true efficiency
Output 20,000 heads per day
The station clock always said, three.

You shoved me into ghetto pens
In Warsaw 10 to every room
Crushed humanity in typhoid and lice
And photographed me for your 'archives'

Zion, where the sun pours down
On everything that lives and grows
Where the child bulges like a grape
And plays, eats ice cream while father prays

161

Burn, burn, burn the streets
Burn the ghettoes house by house
Warsaw's one million murdered eyes
It was photographed for the archives!

The names are jewels in the crown
The Jews will wear with burning pride
Treblinka, Auschwitz, Warsaw, Lodz
Buchenwald, Vilna, Maideneck and Plonsk

The crown is sticky with fresh drawn blood
Its gore refreshed with new victims
This is the punishment for nailing god
To two bits of wood, you evil dogs.

We killed God?! No God forbid!
You did, yes, its all written down
We've got the facts, witnesses, times
Gods only son, what a heinous crime

Get cyclone B gas and watch them writhe
Like scalded snakes, they twist and scream
Tear at the walls with broken nails
They killed god, lets burn them alive

But just suppose he wasn't god
Just suppose he was a man
Jewish, a rabbit, preaching good,
Healing the sick, curing the lame

Then how many rivers of blood were shed
How many lives were thrown away
How much suffering, the millions dead
While Joshua Christ looked on and wept

It's a soft warm day in Tel-Aviv
The cafes crowd up now with noise
The car horns hoot, the angers rise
Oh why can't they be more civilised.

TORY MANIFESTO

SERVANT: Yes Mam, I will paint it grey
I will paint the sun away.
PM: Get those smiles out of my sight
SERVANT: I'll stitch up children's grins alright
PM: That laughter, stop it now you hear
SERVANT: Yes mam, right away don't fear.
PM: I saw a couple holding hands
SERVANT: How dare they do such a thing Mam.
PM: Ban those shows of tenderness
SERVANT: I'll do it, I'll stop that gushy mess.
PM: Make streets straight and morals clean.
SERVANT: Immediately it's done, highness and serene.
PM: Work is not a dirty word.
SERVANT: I'll stitch it in their brains the curs
PM: Queue up like good old british mugs
SERVANT: For what Mam, pray, the dole or pubs?
PM: For serving our good gracious queen
SERVANT: Ah, the army will make their toecaps gleam
PM: Make them believe that might is right
SERVANT: Hates the best way to make them fight
PM: The blacks and the yellows, the reds, the browns
SERVANT: An evil ruining our sweet town!
PM: We need more hate that's packed in bombs
SERVANT: I'll order dozens more, we'll be strong
PM: We must defy the commie threat
SERVANT: We'll scare the people half to death
PM: Spread lies like truth and truth like lies
SERVANT: The usual tory way, your highness
PM: Tits big as melons for the fools
SERVANT: We'll whore out daughters in the daily news
PM: They'll work much harder in factories

SERVANT: Inspired by tits they'll never feel
PM: Still, it gives the working class a thrill
Increase rewards for clever brains
SERVANT: In what way shall the people gain?
PM: Double the prizes in football pools
SERVANT: Inspired! Your highness is no fool
PM: That's what the socialists all lack
SERVANT: The common touch, rob, cheat, attack
PM: We need more goals, find us a cause
SERVANT: Hunt whales, kill seals, lead in petrol, more
   cars.
PM: That's just the start, the merest tip
SERVANT: Cut schools, close hospitals, run down pits
PM: Its getting warmer but what will inspire
SERVANT: A vote from Jesus? What could be higher!
PM: Bravo, I'll pray tonight for his support
SERVANT: Some smashing quotes for our billboards
PM: Like nuclear bombs are good for peace?
SERVANT: I think that love was all he preached
PM: Oh dear, a broody socialist sod!
Cut out the middleman and go to god! (inspired)
SERVANT: With god our side has got to win
PM: Remember how Shakespeare was used by him
SERVANT: God, yes so clever to rape his plays
PM: To justify slaughter every day
Now you my man must choose them well
SERVANT: A vote to labour and you'll go to hell?
PM: Hmm? Something more delicate to inspire the hordes
SERVANT: A vote for Thatcher is a vote for the Lord?
   (eagerly)
PM: Ahhh, remind me when I write the lists
SERVANT: A knighthood would be perfect, Miss
PM: The manifestos done… another day
SERVANT: Well spent your grace, is what I say.
PM: Free enterprise to rob and thieve
SERVANT: (wistful) It's good to have a philosophy.

A BEAST

A baboon is a strange intelligent creature
Living in forests, and swinging from trees
Scaling steep cliffs, stealing honey from bees

In a way not too dissimilar, has similar features
With the hair fluffed out, their eyes closed in
Like a nutty professor or one of our kin,
Even looks like my Uncle Sam
With its long proud nostrils that seem to fan
To two round tunnels on its thoughtful face.
There's even a touch of our own Brian May.
The babies stay close, to their mums they cling fast,
As they forage for food and chew the tree bark,
The young baboons just revel in play,
Leaping and screeching and wrestling all day.

The dad's arses are bulging in purple and red
Like ripened plums, throttled and crushed,
To a female baboon, it stirs her young lust
So delicate, odorous, smelling of musk
She grunts and gurgles and yuk yuk yuk...
Now this baboon loved her tawny brown mate
With his sinewy arms and wobbling gait
His thick coat he wears like a general's cape.
They'd forage together each morning at dawn
For banana and sweet gum until the late morn,
She loved his smell, his grunts and his cock
She loved his lust for her sweet pungent crack
Then after they scrambled, they swung and they played
They rolled in the earth and slept where they lay
Never were creatures so finely attuned
To the life of the forest as these two baboons.

The land was all theirs and the nature was free
The sun and the rain, the hills and the seas
The rivers and vines, spiders and bees,
Giant butterflies and silly chimpanzees
The snake with its coat of shimmering glass
Slithering silently through the long wet grass

But somewhere in somewhere where few trees grow,
Where flowers are scentless and no birds sing
Where lions and tigers don't hunt for their prey
They're thrown slabs of meat behind bars where they stay
Where they stay and pace the floor every day
And baboons and monkeys are kept in small cages
A place where mankind hollers and rages,
Where the beasts of the night go hunting in gangs
And rot-teethed murderers bare their fangs
Where the roar of the creature heaving his guts
Are the sounds of this jungle, while slags vent their lust,
In knee-trembling bunkups at the back of the pub.
In such a strange world did one man stew,
Frustrated, loose-ended, bent over his desk
Spewing out garbage, on his laptop he sweats,
A TV critic who feeds by the shite,
He has to churn out, night after night.
Fine tuning his cretinous, lumbering words
Like a pigeon picking through freshly laid turds.

But he's worth much more than this he thinks,
To write a column week after week
His nose firmly pressed to societies sphincter
Earning a living through mankind's stink.
He had a passion to be a man,
But a man needs a spine to hold him up straight.
How can you give a spine to a snake?
How can you put muscle in jelly?
He rose from his desk, eyes dead and cold
He had an idea that would make him look bold
Yes he had an idea that would make him look bold.

Now the alpha male baboon makes all the decisions
Where to find food, he has instinct and vision,
He grunts and he brays and acts out his dreams
But they know what he's saying 'Let's follow the stream'
Yes they know what he's saying, they know what he
    means
When he grunts and he barks and sometimes he screams

But how could he know, our friendly baboon
How could he know of a beast seeking prey?
A spineless beast whose breath stinks of fear
Who needs to kill you to make his day
Who needs to kill you to see what it's like
Who needs to kill you since he thinks it so brave
Who needs to put you in an early grave
Since this might give him the spine that he craves.

This pathetic beast, this demented dog
But dog is too kind, not even a pig
Not even a rat, but something much lower
Something lower? What could be more base?
Than a human being that cannot feel,
A human being without a spine,
A human being with a need to kill,
To clog his emptiness with a mindless thrill.

The beast he rose from his desk one day,
A potent idea drizzled through his sour brain
How can he become a man?
By trawling through the vomit the gogglebox spews
His spine turned to jelly, his brain turned to goo
But then one day he found the clue
Seek to destroy what you can never create
It makes you feel good, makes you feel strong
So get yourself a fucking gun
Yes! Get yourself a fucking gun.

A soft-nosed 357 blew out his lungs
The lungs of our baboon high up in his tree
The TV critic aimed so carefully.
Two hundred and fifty yards, he was so proud.
'Not a bad shot' he proclaimed aloud.
Hey, now you're a man, now you're real hot!
Tanzania will never be quite the same,
There's one baboon less. The man was so brave.
And then this slug crawled back to his desk
And wrote about his mighty quest.

ELEGY FOR JEANETTE WINTERSON'S RABBIT

Dear rabbit, you were slain poor thing,
For nibbling Jeanette Winterson's herbs,
For such a brazen act of theft,
Dear Fluffy, you were sorely cursed.

You must not gnaw a writers herbs,
Not one so lauded for her prose,
Or else into the steaming pot
You're thrown or served up for Sunday Roast

But since the lady is such a bard,
This feat cannot go unannounced
Your sacrifice must show the world
Just how a naughty rabbits trounced.

With pride all puffed she stews her text
Into the twitters rancid mulch,
So all the world may gawp and gasp,
While down the hatch it goes. One gulp.

Yes, show the world your 'countryways'
With your bold and gore-slimed hands.
How you disembowelled the beast
And, fed its entrails to the cat.

How bravely you skinned the wretched thing
It's lifeless lolling head just stared
Your corpse is bubbling in the pot
To what can bunny be compared...

Ah yes the writers ever fertile brain
Will see a use beside your flesh,
Although the bunnys now been slain
It comes to life... As a glove puppet!

Oh how bright and earthy we are
Red cheeked on country soil,
Knee deep in mud and country stench
While the bunny's entrails boil

Oh how the world did scream and howl
Yes we prefer our corpses wrapped,
Or served with pasta al dente please
In our local bistro or caff.

I'm now a dirty country girl,
Our lauded scribbler proudly cries,
Let me shove it down your throat
Don't live your Waitrose-wrapped city lies.

But others felt the Fluffy's pain
Could see this doe eyed pretty beast
That lives to hop and knaw the herbs
We understand that humans feast

That humans feast on all that moves,
Mankind shall have dominion, we must,
We shoot, we hook, we trap, we skin,
We murder elephants for their tusks

30 million sharks drown for their fins
To feed some lazy scumbags guts,
And whales are murdered in the deep
Cause Japanese Fishermen say, they must

And tigers parts will stiffen cocks
Of those whose brains have long gone soft
And bears are shot in Siberian wastes
By playboys whose souls have turned to rust

So what's a little rabbits life,
That lives to hop and leap about,
Who cares if Miss Winterston takes a knife
And lets his guts come tumbling out,

What was it that touched a soul
To twitter, "never shall I read your words again,
For what you wrote has made me sick"
Oh the words were full of pain

What was it that touched a soul, to squeal
At bunny rabbits sad demise?
Was it the way she crowed with glee
So proud of stealing bunnys life

Was it the way she justified
For nibbling a sprig of parsley – its death
That just a writers poetic bent
We must know that it was meant, in jest.

But yet a sprig of doubt remains
The meerest shadow of some faith
Some fools believe that they're Gods creation
Not just another morsel for us to taste

Oh what a simple view to take,
A little childrens fantasy,
Adoring nature's masterworks
And squeeze them oh so lovingly

Open your big fat stupid mouth,
And crunch down hard and chew and grind
It's what it's there for idiots just a meal
With a real fine rose, mind

And yet, I say, for all of you,
That felt a shudder, whose heart was tapped

Soppy sentimentalists, naïve souls
But it's you we need, so very much.

It's you whose heart bleeds for a rabbit,
You'd have a friend in Shakespeare text
"There is providence in the fall of a sparrow"
Young William wrote for Hamlets death

For fools have what the whole world needs,
Imagination, with mystic wings
Which takes us far above the shuntering herd
Don't weep for bunny you silly thing

FIGHT GAME

I'm gonna fight him and hit him hard.
He thinks he's tuff... he thinks he's strong
But he's just one big tub of lard.
The odds are against me... I'll prove them wrong.
My fists are taped, my gloves laced tight,
I take the long walk to the ring,
This is gonna be my night,
When I knock him out... he'll hear the angels sing.

I'm strolling down with a bit of a bop,
The hands shoot out, they wanna feel
The champs hard body, that's sculpted outta rock
That's sweetly wrapped in muscles of steel.
Their hands whip out to bring them luck.
Get outta my way... buzzing like flies,
All excited when they see me smash...
The world champ into a bowl of mash.

I climb up the steps and into the ring,
Loosen my robe, the crowd all cheer,
Oh boy, I can hear the beating of mighty wings
The angel of death is hovering near
Sniffing the odour of pain in the air,
My opponent is already sweating in fear.
I circle the ring, get the feel of the space.
My head is steady and my purpose is clear

'Touch gloves and fight'... the referee spouts,
We lock eyes with venom so intense
No lovers stared at each other, so devout
No lovers had such passion to vent,

We wanna hurt each other real bad,
But I can taste the fear in his guts,
I can smell defeat in his breathe
So now I'm dancing, JAB, JAB, JAB!

I'm sussing him out… I'm testing his skills,
My hands shoot out like pistons, real fast
Don't rush in, I'm going for the kill,
I'm superman baby and the bum won't last,
He'll not seeing it coming, I move like a ghost
I'm dancing like lightening, he'll get no rest
Till he lay down quietly on the deck,
He won't see it coming, he'll never guess

KA BOOM! KA BLAM! a right hook smashed home
His eyes are widening like a startled hare
He takes a step back, he's on the ropes
KA BAM! KE SMASH! I can taste the fear
Left hook to the ribs, uppercut to the chin
Tries to cover up, raises his gloves real high
I duck real low and bang another in
I hear him groan and the pain says 'Hi'!
I'm atomic power and laser beams,
My protons are swimming, I'm nuclear armed
I'll detonate the champ to the land of dreams
I'll hear him howl and cry for Ma,
Ready now to stick him hard,
He'll bounce off the ropes, I take the streetcar,
Pull my fist right back to the moon,
then let it snap, like a sudden monsoon.

It's moving faster than the speed of light,
Too fast for any mortal man,
But then, but then, an angel slips
Between my fist and this piece of ham,
I miss, not possible, my aim was astute,
How could I miss, how could I fail?

174

How did I not connect with the brute,
How did I not bang, bang on the nail?
Such things, tho rare can manifest
A miniscule slip, a trick of the light,
A heartbeat too fast, he turns in a sec,
My aim was travelling with a might bite,
I overshot the runaway
And expose a perfect space,
A target, now he sees payday,
An opportunity to blow me away.

So as I'm skidding forward, right
Like a dope on a piece of soap,
He left connects with a mighty wham,
A stick of dynamite went ka blam
KA BOOM! KE SMASH! KE SPLAT! KE SLAM!
I went down like a ton of bricks
Darkness fell and stars did their dance
'GET UP! GET UP!' the corner shrieks…!

The referee counts… I'm awake on five!
I stagger to my feet, I'm still alive
My opponent stares, grins like a fiend,
Even hops up and down like he's doing a jive
Take a deep breath and I'm up on eight
'Fight on', the ref wipes down my gloves,
But now my brains on roller skates
And the champs mind is set to auto – destruct!

Bell! Bell! Saved by the Bell!
Did any sound, ever sound so sweet.
I stagger flapping to my seat…
'You've dropped your guard!' my second screams!
While giving me water, mopping up the blood.
'He's laughing at ya, thinks ya made of clay'
'He got ya with a sucker punch, you mug'
'Go for the body, till your head clears. Ok!

Bell! I'm out for the second, gloves held high
Wants to put me out, thinks I'm ready for the kill
But I tap dance away and his punches fly by...
My head has cleared and I'm over the hill.
A tap, a jab, a punch, a clinch
Passing the time, entertaining the mob,
The rounds go by, sure he's ahead by a pinch
But baby, I'm waiting to fell the slob.

Round eight, I get a vision, this is the time.
Don't let him go, this is your night,
The ghost of my heroes... say this is your night...
Joe Louis, Frazier, Tyson and Ali
The Great Marciano and Sugar Ray,
Sony Liston, gone before his time,
As Shakespeare said... 'Summon up the blood,
Disguise fair nature, with hard favoured rage.'

When Ali said, on round number seven,
 gonna send his man straight to heaven
So this is your night... a new world champ,
But he won't go down and its round eleven
I just gotta put out his lamp.
Take a chance... I feint with the left
He blocks with his right and drops his glove
POW! I put one in... ow! I'm so deft
Sweet on the button. Pow! I hit him hard!

A bazooka darlin came from space,
He didn't see it, until too late.
Took him, do you believe in elevation?
He went horizontal, that transubstantiation
His flesh was turned into a block of stone
He looks like he was taking a nap
They dragged him to this corner, he gave a low moan
Throw in the towel, don't be a sap...

But no, he wants to finish, no TKO
He wants to finish on his feet,
He stands up trying to look real mean,
Feel sorry for the bum... but he's gotta go,
Put him out of his misery, knock him out real clean.
He sucks the last shards of energy, man he's got guts,
A right hook taps me gently on the chin,
It felt like a kiss, poor guys, he's going nuts!

Now is the time buddy, say your prayers,
He knows it's coming, but don't wanna go down,
The pride of a champ, not in front of his babe,
She's sitting ringside in a vale of tears,
For a split second I catch her eye,
While I slam him to the ropes and crack his ribs,
'Don't hurt him, don't hurt my baby', she seemed to cry.
He holds me in a desperate clinch.

I would have slammed the bum to the deck,
But something in that moistened eye,
God damn, it held me back, can't see a lady cry,
I've beat him, I've won, don't make him a wreck,
Resists giving him that final crack
So I did, the final bell, he didn't go down
But stayed upright, walked back like a man.
So now, oh yes, I've got the crown.

I am now the heavyweight champ,
Champion of the World, they carry me high,
Shouting and screaming... 'Hey, you're the man!'
We circle the ring, once more I catch her eye,
A split second no more, but it tells me all,
Since under the tears there's a tiny smile,
Tell you the truth, it made me stand tall,
I'm the champ, be magnanimous in another's fall.

'You caught me, with a lucky punch'
He tries now to schmooze,

'I've never gone down in my whole career'
He's grinning under a bloody ooze
He's sprouting from two busted lips,
'Cos you were the best', I said, but I knew why
He wasn't on the way to the garbage tip
Saved by his sweet ladies teardrop in her eye
Now the Champion of the world, I'm proud,
I'll scream to the hills, howl it to the clouds,
Man, you can't fake it in the ring
Get your daddy to give you a hoist,
Fake your way at Uni and get a degree
Whose arse can you lick while it's still moist
In the ring it's what you are, it's what you be,
God bless you Mister, you made history!

THE DIAMOND JUBILEE

The Jubilee, the Diamond Jubilee,
Oh God , that's great, that's smasheroo,
Get out the flags, the bunting, the streets
Of England, up and down, in every town,
Are celebrating this special day,
The trestle tables laid, the cakes are baked,
Kids are shouting, dads are pissed,
And yes, s'not raining, no not yet,
Oh thank you God for blessing this great day
This Jubilee, the Diamond Jubilee,
For on this day, this blessed day,
We kneel, we cry, we pray, yes pray
And say, oh thank you Lord, yes thank you God.,
That's what we want to say, from every mouth
In this great British land we join
Together, linking hands and beery breath
Chatting to our neighbours, yes!
The first time ever that we met,

Though saw you in the aisles of Waitrose
Yes, from time to time, but now
Yes now upon this Diamond Jubilee
We show our rotten teeth and smile
Oh yes, we smile and say, have a sausage mate
Let's celebrate this great and glorious day,
The barbecue is smoking nicely, kids are jumping
Like one great 'lectric current from John O' Groats
To old Southend does link us all,
Yes all of us, us British through and through
The Union Jack flows through our veins
And VAT-free pasties line our guts,

And Tesco's drumsticks scorch and crackle
A million chickens bit the dust,

That precious day, that Diamond day
And Cumberland sausages pop and crack
To celebrate those sixty glorious years
When our great beautiful Queen bestrode the throne
Get cracking duck, your old man's now brown bread,
So get your sweet bum on that throne, my dear
And yes, for sixty splendid years you sat,
Smashed champagne bottles onto new-born ships,
Opened hospitals and welcomed dodgy prats
From far-off lands and made them feel at home,
To show, we know, oh yes, we know
They torture their own people, kill off dissidents
But look, we bear no grudges, 'cause
They've also a crown upon their head.

So let's forget all that this day,
This once and special day, this Diamond day,
And put an armada on the smoky Thames,
A cavalcade of everything that floats,
Barges, worn-out tugboats, ships with sails,
Fluttering a joyous welcome on the wind,
Whilst you, yes you, our glorious Majesty,
Sail down between them, Boadicea,
On your golden craft that slides
Between the naughty choppy little waves,
Each wave bowing as you pass,
In all your splendour, all your dignity
Standing upright with your stalwart bloke Prince Phil
Not sitting on your blood-red thrones oh no,
You're made of sterner stuff than that,
By God, you're made of England's blood and soil,
So grit those pale grey teeth and bear the biting cold,
Whilst all the nation gripping plastic flags,
Stand and wave and wave and stand,

All straining just for a peek, bladders bursting
'Where's the bloody loos?' No matter,
Here's our wondrous, blessed, glorious Queen,
'Oh look, by heck she's waving to us,
Yes she moves an arm from side to side,'
And tried so valiantly to smile,
But God, it's hard, it's hard to stretch those lips,
Into a semblance of a grin...

Imagine if you will, her view,
The sight of all those thousands of bobbing heads
Rain-dashed and bitter cold, yet chanting
Those old and moving patriotic songs
About a land of hope and glory...
Shedding even then some salty tears,
Whilst heaving up their guts in the stewy Thames
Who could smile, yes, who could force, even a grin,
Ramrod straight she stands, will not be moved
Frozen like a marble obelisk
While Phillip's dying to take a piss...

But you, oh people of noblest England,
Fastened to your TV screens like flies
That buzz around some rancid meat.
Hoping, yes hoping that against all odds,
Her majesty our darling Queen,
Will grace us with a trembling nod,
And please, oh please ma, just a smile – Oh yes! Just that,
Would cause the sullen sun to hide,
His face, for how could he compare,
Yes how, to her majesties radiant smile, so fair
But still, yes still she thrusts right through
Old father Thames, where even now
A salmon might point its nose, so pink
And not shrink away with horror at the stink
Since it's now almost (but not quite) fit to drink
But still, gallantly she stands and stares,

And still her smile is masked by thoughtful clouds
The nation, standing, waving, shrieking, hoping
That any moment that great beam will come
Those wine red lips will part and then, yes then
Her smile will break the nation's heart.

The well-wrapped BBC chaps fasten TV lens
They must not miss, that moment, that moment
Of sheer bliss when she conveys to all of us
The love she feels for all, the rich and stinking poor.
And so keen are they to view the sight
On which a hundred TV lens are trained
That now, in innocence and faith,
They start to make up what she feels
'Oh look' they say, how happy she seems, our Queen
'Oh look' they gasp, she seems so pleased,
'I do believe a smile escaped her lips'
'Oh yes, oh yes, I'm sure it was, weren't you?'

Of course it was, or was it just a shadow that fell,
But no matter, now it's over and this Diamond day
Is done, this once and special day is printed
On our minds for evermore, this day -
And when we're old and grey we'll tell
Our children, tell them, seated by the fireside
We saw the Queen of England on her barge
Like Cleopatra on the Nile and at the end
She gave us all one great ginormous smile.

FOR HER WITHOUT A NOSE

You saw it, so did I, we all did,
We all saw it, not quite believing,
Who could believe it? No one could...
No one. Cause quite frankly it was
Unbelievable... That... That... That
Human beings could do such a thing...
Could carry out such an act...
Such a bestial, such a horrible
Thing... That human beings,
Only by name mind you, only by name.
Nothing human in them except... Remotely.
Since savage dogs do such things, only
Savage... wild... filthy, stinking,
Vicious hyenas... or... ok... human trained dogs
Could do such a thing, such an unbelievable,
Dastardly, such a noxious, such a bestial,
Such a monstrous thing!
What? You ask, what? What is it? This thing,
That is almost, almost impossible to say,
To write, to set down, to record,
To give voice to, to put into words,
To speak... no words should shape those
Abominations, no lips should give them sound,
You can't, you really just can't,
You saw it. In the papers... that's where you saw it,
That's where you saw it,
Your stomach turned over, your heart swelled
And skipped a beat, your soul writhed
And shrieked, acid trickled into your mouth, but
You couldn't give words to it... could you?
You could only point, just point... Just say

To whoever is within your hearing,
Oh! Oh! Oh! Oh! Oh! My God!
Look… look at this… yuk!
Oh my fucking Christ, look at this!
What fucking, holy mother of Christ!
What disgusting, loathsome, subhuman beast…
But you couldn't find words for it
Could you? Eh? Could you?

You know what I am talking about?
Of course you do, you know, you know really,
Cause you saw it, you saw it, and what you saw
You cannot name, cannot describe… ever…
Just point, just, if you can, point… say…
Look at this… this… this thing, this is,
This is… the words come hard, even the words
On the edge of the event… not the thing itself
Just the stain at the edge.

Of the puddle of blood, just
Clues to the vile act.. You see it's so hard,
So hard to say, for what you say, you bring
It all to life, but you have to… for her,
For this her, this woman, you have to, for
That woman whose face, whose once beautiful face
A beautiful woman's face, moulded, shaped, sculptured
Over time immemorial to arrive at such perfection
After such a time when centuries fell like leaves,
Until she, this woman arrived here,
With her intelligent beautiful face.
That she had, that she, this woman
This lovely young and perfect woman
Hand-made by the fingers of God with all
Those fine elements that define what
It is to be human, that perfect symmetry
And grace, that she had until… some low, fetid,
Stinking human rat, but no sound, even

Those sucked up from the bogs of hell
From the slimy drains and ducts of hell,
Could ever fit you, could ever
Describe the crawling abomination that is man. Man,
Is that not foul enough? Yes, that must do,
Man!!!!

So this is what the picture says,
It shows what is inside the soul of
Man who lives in hell, it shows his mighty works
For amongst the whispering butterflies, amongst,
The dazzling creatures of the sea.
Amongst all that is wondrous, and divine,
Amongst the swift and dazzling cheetah, the
Heaven soaring eagle, the intrepid flying fox,
The gargantuan singing whale, lay the anomaly
Of man.
He grips his filthy knife and cuts off
The nose, that's what he does, he
Chops, he slashed off her nose, her beautiful,
Her tender woman's nose, as punishment for
Wishing to escape from this filthy man / beast
For wishing to escape his filthy stink,
His sour breath, his dull and stupid speech
His filthy fingers, his raw scabrous tongue,
His idiot's eyes, his belchy devils stomach,
His idiots chatter, his nighttime stench,
So he cuts off her nose, to prove to himself
He can be as foul, as sinister and as loathsome
As she could ever dare to believe.
So now there is a hole in the centre of her face,
That's what he did, that's what we saw,
That's what the picture shows, that's what is
So hard to speak, but so very necessary to speak
What are these men who can hold a young woman
Down, are they from the sperm of Satan, what stinking
    effluvium

185

Runs through their veins, what sewage was their mother's
    milk?
And who will stop them?

Yes, a man did this and doesn't that shame us
To be called a man? Doesn't it?

Your time will come mister, your time will come,
And when you least expect it your time will come
Or every foul act you will reap
A thousand fold,
For every cruel and most unnatural act
You perpetrate you will tighten
The cords of the worlds hate,
Around your throat until your breath
Is squeezed out drop by drop
And what is left is just some foul junk,
Too foul even for the earth which shuddering
Vomits it out, but then the vultures will
Come, for them you'll be rancid snack!

MOHAMMED

Bangalore: a two-and-a-half year old boy Mohammed
Munir was defecating by the side of a poorly-lit lane on
Tannery Road in KG Halli early on Thursday morning,
when a truck ran over him.

The Sunday times of India, Bangalore, March 28, 1999

Poor Mohammed was taking a roadside crap.
The night in India was warm and soft,
Urine sweet and mixed with diesel fumes,
Mo's tummy was tight as a Major's drum
He sniffed the familiar damp and acrid air
So young but knew enough to lift the shreds
That barely covered his young marble cheeks.
Mama was snoring in her makeshift bed,
Which was her sanctuary, a piece of street,
They'd both ate well that night, some treasured meat,
Lucky bonus from a restaurant's plate,
Dug up from the mines of a garbage heap.

A tired truck driver, sleep still thickly caked
His eyes, bumps down the twilight dusty road,
The familiar thundering, honking beast
Squealed loud beneath its heavy load.
His eyes search for the pavement's broken edge,
But it has crumbled into the killing street,
The music's on some sickly sweet refrain,
The window's down, the air thins out the heat,
In wafts the stinking smells of human pain
But he can't smell the young Mohammed's meat.
But soon Mohammed hears the roaring,
Hears the engine growl, the headlights boring

Through the early blood-red dusty morning
Two panther eyes stare dumbly, blindly out
And lit the lump of fragile human flesh
Before it him; knocked the shit
Right out, just when the child Mohammed sighed
With sweet relief, just then the burning lights
Of young Mohammed Munir swiftly died.

NIRMALA AND DES RAJ

Dalit lovers publicly killed, 'cremated'.

In a brutal act reminiscent of the medieval times, two
young Dalit lovers were publicly killed at Shimla village
in the district of Haryana yesterday for having dared to
elope. Des Raj was 23 and Nirmala was 17. Nirmala
was attacked with a sharp-edged weapon which was
repeatedly thrust into her stomach. Des Raj was stoned
to death. The bodies were then set on fire. No arrests
have been made so far.

Express News Service, Kaithal. March 30th, 1999

There is a place called Shimla, which is cursed
For now, for ever to eternity
And every hand that gripped a stone or stick
Shall be abhorred in the eyes of God
For now, ever to eternity
The dirty, stinking fists that gripped the knife
That plunged into the holy innocent flesh
Of poor Nirmala shall be cursed until
Their seed dies out with their infected line
Since nothing pure can sprout from poisoned blood
For now, forever to eternity.

Des Raj, young man and full of sublime love
Did cast his spell and on Nirmala's heart
Which is the basis of the universe.
Love is the sacred balm the links our race
It celebrates creation, is the nurse
Who heals, and makes us human not mere beasts

Love is god's highest gift so rare it yearns
To find its image in another's face.
So Des found in Nirmala's eyes his soul
Nirmala found in Des's eyes her soul.

This is the purpose of God's plan for us,
Since we are echoes of the universe.
The way the lonely moon find its own face
Upon the rolling sea and yearning tides,
The way the night spills itself into the day
The thirsty tree opens its arms to rain
All giving, loving, feeding, nourishing,
All caring, nursing, holding, cherishing.
Love binds the endless stars into their place
And he or she that seeks to cut that chord
Shall be accursed all their living days.

And he or she that seeks to destroy the gift
That god bestows to help his master plan
Will be as one, who stops the blessed rain,
Or rips the nourishing sun from out the sky.
Or tears the sacred love from out two breasts
A curse will fall upon their evil heads
Since no one dare a precious life unthread,
You have no right, no cause to murder life
Because two lovers found each other's souls.
So jealously insane you took your knives
And tried to cut their love from out their hearts
But love had fled and all they left behind
Were just two lumps of torn and bleeding flesh.

For Des and his Nirmala are one
United, sitting by God Krishna's side,
While Jesus heals their wounds in paradise.

ANITA

Husband, in-laws get 7 years imprisonment for dowry death. Barely four months after her marriage to Vijay, Anita committed suicide as she was unable to bear the continuous harassment by her husband and his parents for not bringing enough dowry.

Hindu Times, April 1st, 1999

They say that Indian women are afraid
Of something worse than foulest dragon's breath
Worse by far than leprosy, plague or death
These noble sari'd creatures wrapped in silk,
Resembling the most exotic plumed birds
Do far the reptile beast with vicious claws,
The dreadful fearsome bitch that spawned her man,
The son-adoring, greedy mother-in-law!

Or like precious moths that stray too near the flame
This bride did fly too near the dragon's maw
And felt the spiteful scorching mother's tongue
Screeching for more silk, more dowry, more!
The bride's thin father was like sugar cane
That had been sucked and almost chewed to death
And had no flavour left to give the son
Whose greed howled like his mother's in on breath
So one dark night an 'accident' occurred
It seems to happen frequently out here
Poor Indian moth was scorched up in their hate
Those wretched gas cylinders are to blame
Ma-in-law says… 'there's more fish in the sea'
As they lowered the charred remains into the grave.

S.U.V (HIP HOP)

I'm just wild about my lovely S.U.V,
I love the size of my shiny black beast
I love the power pouring into me.
S.U.V S.U.V S.U.V
Selfish, ugly, vandal me
Cause that's what I am, you'd better believe,
S for selfish, that's the way to be
U for ugly, that's my brute you see
V is for vandal cause I don't give a damn,
If I pour my filth all over the land
If I pour my filth all over the land
If my thirsty big truck heats up the air,
By burning up the juice, cause I don't care
As long as I can satisfy my desire
T'sall that matter, I aint no liar
Don't wanna be good, don't wanna be green,
My money is clean, though my soul is stained
So I wanna sit in my S.U.V
Shut the fuck up and let me be.

Then one fine day, ain't no gasoline left,
Oil wells are empty and the earths a stinking mess
But I'm sitting here still in my S.U.V
Pretending that we're going on a holiday
The tyres are flat, the body's full of rust
The window wipers broken and the air condition's bust,
But I don't give a damn cause I'm deaf, dumb and blind
To anything or anyone that isn't mine, mine
Cause greed my baby is the name of the game.
So come inside my S.U.V and then we all can play.
Take the wheel baby, we'll go for a drive,
So let's pretend honey that we're still alive!

A BRONX SCHOOL TEACHER WAS SHOT IN THE CROSSFIRE BETWEEN TWO DRUG DEALERS

A Bronx school teacher bites the dust
At fifty-three she lived alone,
Her parakeet her solitary pal,
She chats to him and cleans his cage,
Then works at public school fifty-three
There she unfurls the mysteries
That lurk in Shakespeare's braided verse,
Audrey Chasen is her name
Not too pretentious, not too bold,
A name that's simple, full of hope,
Her parents were two modest souls
When they imposed upon their child
A name that has the faintest taint
Of maiden, teacher, worthiness
Audrey, destined to make the headlines
Although she lived with a parakeet
And taught the rhythms in Shakespeare's beat
Two gutless gunmen, soul soured up,
Their brains burnt down to charcoal heap
By crack, greed, fear, illiteracy
Who knew not Shakespeare from a boom box beat
Their dull cells blinked in darkest ooze
That once God destined to be a brain
Enough volts there to fire a gun.

Between the two foul gangster's slugs
The innocent Audrey's car slid by
Her head still singing out the sounds

193

That Shakespeare spake four centuries past
The words that pour sweet unguents on
The wounded souls that need his balm.
She heard within her solitary life
The violence of the Yankee world
Yet wished to pour into the dragon's maw
Into the festering and stinking jaws
Into the rabid hell-hole of The Bronx
Essence of tranquillity and love,
'Were I a glove upon that hand
That I might touch that cheek'
The bullets crashed into her skull and bones
Turned Audrey Chasen into minced meat.

So Audrey's now wired up, pulse weak
Thoughts scattered by the bullets' whine
That ricocheted around her head
So full of midsummer night's dream
'I know a bank where the wild thyme blows'
The steel chews and tears up the flesh,
'Where oxslips and the nodding violets grows'
Blood spurts, veins rip like telephone lines,
Shattered by the tempest rage
'There sleeps Titania some time of the night,
She clings to life in her white grave',
The crossfire of a gunfight was her fate,
Not 'to be or not to be'
More...'The readiness is all'

Who will feed the parakeet she quests
Dear Audrey lying in her bower,
'Shall I compare thee to a summer's day?
 Thou art more lovely and more temperate.'

SMOKE

Go on, have another smoke,
Suck another fag,
Fill your veins with tar,
Till your lungs are rags.

Flappin' in your chest
Desperate to suck air
But those sacks are full of holes
And you ain't even got a spare.

Just like a worn out bag-pipe
Full of rips and rents,
It squeaks when you try to squeeze it,
And it never gonna mend

You're wheezing when you try,
So hard to climb the stairs,
Puffing like a rusty train
That's on its final legs.

At last you reach the top step
Grip the bannister like steel.
Your gnarly knuckles, bloodless white,
Oh you badly want to pee.

Just a few more steps to go,
Puff, pant, squeak, gasp, hiss.
Ok, unzip, your dong is out
Oooh! It badly wants to piss

Just stand there quivering,
Like a leafless dying tree,
Dreaming of times long gone past
When peeing was ecstasy

Now the carbon's thickened your tubes,
The pee dribbles slowly out
Drippin', drippin', please, a few drops more.
Just about strain it out.

Few more steps to the bedroom door,
Aaaah, just plonk down on the bed,
On the bedside table, tobacco, cigarette papers,
Ok, roll a thick one for resting my head.

I roll real good, lick the paper's edge,
Stick it between my lips,
Light it, suck the first familiar brew,
Wow! Goes straight to my head..

Cough, cough, splatter, spit,
Always on the first bloody drag
Just the lungs begging, 'leave them alone!'
But on the second there's no more nag,

Suck, suck. Blow, blow, the tip's a bold red eye.
It burns, my larynx squirms,
But I'm feeling mighty fine,
Shame the effing cost's so high!

My bedroom stinks like a waiting room,
In railway stations of the past.
In its rancid air I sleep and squeak
Don't know how long I can last..

Got through the night in chokes and gasps,
And shreds of sleep were few

Morning comes, dig the crust from my eyes
And gob in the spittoon.
Oh God, I need a fag, real bad,
I turn to roll a snout
The ashtray's full of ancient butts,
Like death has spat them out,

Never mind, I pull a tiny sheet,
Sprinkle my beloved weed,
But hacks and coughs disturb my hands
And I spill the precious seed.
Ok, I crawl into the carpet shag,
I rescue bits and scraps
But it's mostly cat hair and dust
Never mind it will do to make a fag.

I light once more and suck it down,
But my lungs won't take no more
Cough and choke and spit and hack,
That's the end, my throat's ripped raw.

It's getting dark, although it's morn
You just took your last breath,
So be quiet now and close your eyes
You don't need fags when you're dead..

ON SALOME IN NEW YORK

New York. Oct. 1995.
The driver said to me, 'Where to?'
I slid behind the dirty shield,
The Perspex wall 'tween man and me,
In case crack-starved I pull a piece
And spread his brains upon the seat.
So now my criminal lust is caged
Behind his battered carapace.

I read the posters on the screen
Which state my rights and not to tip
Unless I'm fully satisfied that
The driver's done his best and been polite,
Taken me by the route I like.
I slump back in my grimy seat
Bandaged up with insulting tape
Like the cab's been wounded, slashed and raped.

New York is held together by
A million miles of this grey tape
Without it, it would fall apart
And crumble in the filthy lake
It seals the rents inside my room
Where the air-conditioned unit smashed
A hole into the hotel wall
The tape fills in the gaping cracks.

The filthy cab lurches and bumps
Like a ship on stormy seas
We bounce along the callused face
Of Manhattan's scarred up streets.

I read my rights, stare at his head,
Tear down Broadway to Brooklyn Bridge,
He's seen this sight a million times
I turn and it's a wonderland.

The city hits the water's edge
It stands quite still and blinks a bit
Like deciding what to do
Whether to try and make the leap.

We hear the bandaged city shriek
From time to time like some poor beast
As yet another knife is thrust
Into its bleeding rotting flanks.

We head down Brooklyn: De Kalb Ave
A name which seems to suit the place
A hairdresser was killed last night
While riding in his cooped up cab

Two gunmen forced his cab open
Like opening a can of beans
And shot to death the man inside
Who read his rights upon the screen
And decided not to tip
Unless the ride was satisfactory
In De Kalb he tipped his blood
Over the cabman's bandaged seats

I stop, get out and kill some time,
And go to where the slaughtered beasts
End up between two slabs of rye,
A pile of pickles on your plate.
JUNIORS, palace of delicatessen
Museum of the ancient tongue,
I sit upon unbandaged seats
The menu is a mile long.

The Talmud of the kosher world
Aromas seep into my world
I'm swaddled in the ghost of ma
Smiling as her wolfish son
Wolfs down her golden fried fish cakes.
So now I order chicken soup
With giant matzo ball within

I slurp the soup, the memory's right!
Divide a sandwich though, it's huge,
A corned beef mountain sheared in two,
One half I donate to my friend,
My tongue begins the steep ascent
My teeth tear footholds in the flesh,
Alas too much, I tumble down,
And divide my half once again.

But now after I crunched the pickles,
And fed my guts, now feed my eyes,
The clientèle is mostly black,
Who come in every shape and size,
Big and small and huge and wide,
Old and young, and mums with babes,
They love the Jews for just one thing
A giant slab that's called cheesecake
Well satisfied we walked the streets,
To warm up before we hit the stage,
We enter a buckled metal door
The rectum to the empty space
Where actors enter to prepare a face,
To meet the faces that they meet
In the theatre's belly we will stew,
But this time we're the delicatess,
The high priced punters get to eat!

A tiny room becomes my cell,
A lonely time, the make-up's cool,

It's forty minutes before I go on,
Those forty minutes feel like hell
My purgatory until I face
A thousand judges in the dark,
Ready to sentence me to death
Or else bravo me into space.

We enter the arena stage
And spin our tale again of pain
Decapitation, lust and death,
In slow motion and stately pace,

I say my final line, my heart is high
From 2000 hands it rained applause
And bravos shattered the Brooklyn skies
At last New York was Salom-ised.

ELEGY FOR JOSH BOWMAR

Elegy for a big black bear:

Where is your Soul,

Josh Bowmar and wife Sarah
Never forget that name Josh Bowmar
Let it be in your brain forever stained
This poor excuse for a human
This bane upon the human race
Josh Bowmar should from his mother's womb been
   scraped
Before he sucked one breath of the earth's precious air.
This putrid lump of human tripe this white trash
Threw his spear, yes hurled his damned spear
Into a living bear, 28 stones 7 foot black bear
A beautiful, 7 foot black bear, you useless piece
Of scum Bowmar and your filthy wretched woman
This pathetic excuse for a woman.
This miserable excuse for a bitch. She herself, slew a
Bear the day before with bow and arrow!
From whence came evil like you from what pestilential
   womb.
From whence, the worthless cesspit inside your skull
What demon poisoned your soul, made it an abattoir
And poisoned your wife, dear Sarah, who
So proudly shot a bear with bow and arrow!
"I'm Tarzan you Jane." You sad lump of humanity
Oh what courage to murder a defenceless animal.
Oh you feel brave to kill a beautiful beast
Oh you're so brave, so butch, so manly, so virile

But you're not, you're a weak, pathetic sicko, you're a
    pervert,
And you're a slob, your wretched dirty wife is a whore to
The devil...
Bowmar what had that bear done to you, what had the
Great beautiful creature done to you, except exist, in all
    its glory,
What, why, how could you, why could you destroy
    something as
Beautiful. It doesn't belong to you, you spineless excuse
    for a male.
What had that magnificent creature done to you?
It was my bear, mine not yours, it was our bear
Ours, not yours, what filthy wretched nation spawned
    such slugs
As you, I know your wretched society can produce a
Diseased brained scum-bag like Trump,
Only a sickly society could even think of offering this
    Micky Mouse wretch one vote.

Even the evil spawn of Trump, even this moron's
    off-spring
His own children go out and kill; his own son shot dead a
Beautiful leopard, tells you everything, doesn't that tell
    you everything,
It does, it tells you everything
Did no parent tell him to hold the beasts of the world
    in awe,
Did no mother
Or father take you to the zoo, show how wonderful and
    precious
Are these creatures, did no one tell you,
What a loathsome piece of pus you are
How could you know, you murdering slug.
You destroyer of the precious treasures of this world.
You did nothing to create this magnificent animal

You gave nothing, you couldn't even revere it, you couldn't even
Hold it in awe, you couldn't gasp as you witness his magnificence.
All you could do is, kill it!
That all you could do you spawn of Satan
Even the simplest human seeing a wounded animal will feel for it
Even a child will weep for a wounded cat, even a brute will
Relieve a creature's pain, but not people like you, not you the
Diseased brained hunter. Who took compassion away for you Bowmar
And your wretched skank of a wife?
Who never taught you to respect the animal treasure of the world,
Are you brain washed on computer games, is taking of a life games?
It was to the Nazis,
The Nazis were brain-washed to be like you Bowmar and your stupid
Piece of garbage called Sarah your wife Bowmar...did you love buying
Your bow Sarah? Was it a strong bow, strong bow hard metal
And you were so thrilled with your beautiful new weapon, and you
Practised, not Chopin, not the jolly japes of Scott Joplin
Anything that might strike one single cell of feeling in you,
Since, there is not one cell, not a scintilla of a cell, the newspaper
Says you compete in the "bikini category of fitness competitions"...
Of course you do.

But Bowmar out of your filthy wretch polluted mouth
 came your
Two cents philosophy, the scumbag's credo, 'critics of
 hunting
Should be ashamed of themselves for trying to kill a
 heritage
That has existed for over a million years'...Oh Mr
 Bowmar
Bless your shit stained heritage, bless your contemptible
Barbarism, you damnable heritage, you nasty
 abomination of a
Human being...if only my words were barbs, were shafts
 of steel,
To put you and your bikini witch into the grave where
 you
Have put this beautiful bear, Bowmar you are forever
 contaminated,
Forever known as a scourge of the earth...
No, Bowmar and wretched repellent bug Sarah you
 should be ashamed,
Ashamed to take one more breath on this beautiful
 earth, ashamed
To contaminate our magnificent world. And all of you,
 mental
Retards who take a weapon and cut short the life of some
 innocent
Animal, all of you who book your plane tickets and put
 on your
Stupid hunting gear, you who are utterly useless
 wretched of
The world, you will be cursed, today, every day and
 forevermore...

SILENCE

Silent your breath,
Or nearly, just a faint
Susurrus... a whisper
Barely, faintly... nearly silent
In silence she appears,
In silence she grows, All
those years ago. She
Reappears in your silence
Untrammelled... delicate aura
She returns on a mist of
Silence. Petals unfold in silence.
You lay, you sleep, in silence
And in silence your dreams
Silently carry you across worlds,
Across time, in silence.

In silence is my body,
My blood flows in silence
My heart beats silently
Unless you press your ear
To my sleeping chest, silent
My cat sleeps in silence, so
Silent as he crawls into his
Sleep, my cat carves out the silence
I awake in silence
Until the sound begins.

The sounds crumble the silence,
The sounds penetrate
The windows, the choking of
Car exhausts... the coughing of trucks.

The screams, squealing tyres
The howling of horns, the
Whining of brakes, the screeching of
Dinosaurs, is how it sounds,
The torture of police sirens,
Tearing the fabric of silence
And then you open your eyelids
And the dream, vision, evaporate
Dwindles, melts, disappears.

But the silence will return,
It will return,
You will find the silence,
You will go to where the silence
Falls, like snowflakes,
Will go to where the only sound
Is the sighing breath of the wind
The whisper of the grass
The slow buzz of the dragonfly
The silence when you pause,
And see the sleeping silence of your child,
But then, when it is the time
When the last tick of the clock
The last thin whisper of breath,
The last heave of your chest
The last flicker of your pulse
The last sigh, the final sound
And then silence, you merge
With the universe,
Your cells with stardust
And move together, silently
In darkness, peace, silence
Eternal silence forever and ever
And ever.

SONGS

MOSLEY'S SONG

We don't want black men or jews
Yellow, red, brown or blue
And lets kick out the homos too
Hitler had the right ideas
Don't knock him son, you need him here
You know you like the uniform
Black boots smashing up your rear
The swastikas just another cross
Reshaped a little here and there
We can nail your hands to that
If you don't stick them in the air

Fascism is here to stay
Trains on time regular pay
Jobs for all the Christian whites
Hate's the best fuel to win our fight
Hate's the way to clean the land
Hate in church and hate in school
Hate at home and hate in your hand
Give me your ignorant, your unemployed, your thick
We'll give you black shirts, boots and sticks

I PRAY IN A SYNAGOGUE

I pray in a synagogue
A synagogue
A synagogue
I pray in a synagogue
Every single day

I pray to almighty god
Almighty god
Almighty god
I pray to almighty god
And this is what I say

I vant to be a rock and roll star
Wear thousand dollar suits
And have a Rolls Royce with a bar
Top models for my lovers
And ten million in the bank
And face on all the covers
And fifty million fans
So...

I pray in a synagogue
A synagogue
A synagogue
I pray in a synagogue
Every single day
I pray to almighty god
Almighty god
Almighty god
I pray to almighty god
And this is what I say

I vant to be a rock and roll star
Wear diamonds on my fingers
And a house in Zanzibar
Madonna for my girlfriend
And a pad in Malibu
Paul Newman for my neighbour
And a gigantic swimming pool!

I pray in a synagogue
A synagogue
A synagogue
I pray in a synagogue
Every single day
I pray to almighty god
Almighty god
Almighty god

I pray to almighty god
And this is what I say
I vant to be a rock and roll star
And sing like Roger Daltry
And play a mean guitar
Hot for me
The just adore my screen test
They're screaming for my hits
And it's champagne for breakfast
Wanna strut like Jagger
And smash my guitar like Pete
Sell 50 million records
And have the whole world at my feet

ROCK AND ROLL STAR

I want to be a rock and roll star
Singing in a palace, glitter lights
A flashy car
I want ten thousand pairs of eyes
All feasting upon me
A mike, a voice, that thrills, a million volts
That's ecstasy

Smash it! Hit it!
Now let's go, guitars on fire
PI/AN/OS
Tongue and chords
And hips and teeth
I tear the air
I hit the beat
Ten thousand hearts
They rise and fall
They pound the rhythm
Hear my call.
I sing. I howl.
I shriek and moan
I'm a rock and roll star
I stand alone.

I want to be a rock and roll star
Diamonds, rubies, silken rags, a Rolls Royce
With a bar
I want to shimmer softly
I wiggle
Grind, yes drive them mad
The crowd roars as I come on stage
Chartreuse, pink and feeling bad

Shout it! Scream it!
Open throats
Feel like a panther
Hit all the notes
I'll send them to heaven
I'll hurl them to hell
My voice is a demon
Cause I'm fuelled by the devil
I sing, I howl
I shriek, I moan
I'm a rock and roll star
I stand alone

I want to be a rock and roll star
My room in Tufnell Park
Is very very very far
I work in Woolworths 9 to 6
I'm getting bored to death
I'm dying on my feet
Oh help, I want to use my breath
To sing
To leap
To run
To fly
Ten thousand hearts
To make them sigh
To soar
To shriek
To shout
To moan
I'm a rock and roll star
And stand alone.

ICE CREAM

I wanna chew it
And suck it
And eat it
Wanna feel it
Wanna taste it
Wanna drink it
Wanna hug it
Wanna sip it
Nice and slow
And caress it
And mess it
Wanna bite it
Kiss it
Lick it clean
And drink the last drop of it
Wanna dive right right right
Down
Into my icecream sundae

I wanna eat it
Wanna taste it
How I miss it
It ain't funny
Oh oh oh oh oh!
How I love it
Love the flavours
And the colour is
So varied/you choosa
What you like and
The tastes are so
Fantastic

Oh it's gorgeous
Oh it's lovely
Wanna dive right right right down
Into my ice cream sundae

I'm a simple
I'm the same
I wanna just
The one I had
Before/its special
And a lovely
Why should I change
I could not ask for more
I'm a hooked
This tastesa good
I'll have the same
And more and more
Wanna hold it
And taste it a
And a chew it
And forever more
I wanna dive right right right
Down in my sundae

TON UP!

I hate driving on the fly-over
Cause I'm not a ton up kid
I'm an easy driver (fast)
I want to cruise along the motorway
Feel the trees and forests
And smell the rain

Don't wanna smash, crash, bam,
Deaddown-headlights on.
Mouth full of flies, screaming hot tyres (fast)
Doing a ton/overtake
And make a mistake
Cars are coming/do I have time
Get back in line/heart a thumping

I wanna see the cows
And hear the lambs
Watch the sun set on a field of corn
Feel my lady's fingers gripping
Squeezing me tight (fast)
And swallow dives and there's a crow
It's a beautiful sight (fast)

Don't wanna growl, screech, skid
Ba boom/be a burn-up boy
Gross intrusion means a head on collision,
And you're a crunched up toy
Don't wanna be king/turn on the speed
A hundred and more
Death makes a killing
If you are willing
That's the end of your joy

I hate driving on the motor way
Lets glide through the hills (fast)
Who needs thrills/just a sunny day
See the river, watch the streams, a swallow dives
The wind on your face
The soft rain to taste
I wanna be A L I V E!!

I CAN'T MAKE UP MY MIND UP

I can't make up my mind if I love you enough
To say the pretty things you want to hear
I can't make up my mind – let's just go on
The way we're doing up to now my dear

Don't force me to speak
Don't cry on the phone
Don't call me a freak
Don't shriek, don't moan

If I can't make up my mind if I love you enough
To say the pretty things you want to hear
If I can't make up my mind – let's just go on
The way we're doing up to now my dear

Love will come, it will grow
Don't trample on the flowers
Let it be – let it be
Can't you see, don't hassle me

If I can't make up my mind if I love you enough
To say the pretty things you want to hear
If I can't make up my mind – let's just go on
The way we're doing up to now my dear
Don't shriek – don't moan
Don't take an overdose
Don't, don't, don't, don't, don't, don't, don't, don't, don't,
    don't, don't...
If I can't make up my mind if I love you enough
To say the pretty things you want to hear

GOING FOR A WALK

Going for a walk walk
Clear the air,
Get the wind in my hair
Going spare
Going insane
Same old thought
Rocking my brain.
Get the dog
Off the rug
Come on Pluto
Wuff Wuff!

We're going for a walk walk
Stretch your legs
Kick those bugs
Out of your head
Get the sun
On your cheeks
Feel the earth
Under your feet
Left right
Right left
I love walking best!

Don't wanna stop at home
Don't wanna be alone
Looking out the window pane
Goin crazy or insane
Will she ring or will she won't
My head full of do and don't
I gotta get outta my head

Open the door, get out of bed
So I'm going for a walk walk

Repeat.

THE MADMAN

The madman walks up and down
No one speaks to him
The madman walks up and down
He howls at the moon
No one speaks to him

Will you buy me a breakfast, he begs
They shake their shampooed heads
They're afraid of his power
They're afraid of his power
They chew their muffins instead
They filled him full of coloured pills
To make him straight like us
Reduce his vision and make him ill
And turn his wild brain to rust

And still the madman walks up and down
His face is thin and gaunt
The madman is the son of man
He once was a child
But now he is wild
No one speaks to him

God change can you spare?
I had a mother too somewhere
I did not come out of a devil's mouth
But took grades at high school, ate ice cream
And had some of the dreams that you had too

And still the madman walks up and down
No one speaks to him

Eating their breakfast in cafes
He passes by a ghostly shade
No one dares speak to him

You who sit safely at home
Eat guacamole by the answer phone
State out of your well-lit window, and behold
A devil raging out there in the cold
Take another mouthful - don't let him take hold
Of your soul
Don't let pity inspire you – lest you lose the
Sanctuary of your well-lined central heated hole

Let him walk up and down
Please don't speak to him
Lest in doing so you might be contaminated
By pity, compassion, rage, softness, generosity
And all other feelings which line your soul and
Are kept in a room, locked up
And festering from lack of air
Open the door, open it if you dare
But if you don't turn to face
The suffering of the human race
Your home will be a cosier place
And still the madman walks up and down
No one speaks to him
Peers in the dustbins, drenched in the showers
Pulls out the roots and eats the flowers
Grows strong in the sun and renews his powers
And howls at the moon
No one speaks to him.

STOP IT

I don't want to be here
To fry alive
I don't want to be her
When a thousand sun lit
Up the sky
I don't want to be here
To hear my children cry
When ten million tons of
Rubble bury us alive
I don't want to see black rain
Falling from the sky

Don't protect me you megaton
Don't protect me you neutron
Don't protect me you hydrogen
Don't protect me you moron
I'd rather die.

Don't want my skin falling off
Don't want my hair falling out
Don't want my blood to boil
Don't want my brain to melt
Don't want the trees to die
Don't want the seas to rot
Don't want the flowers to end
Don't want your foul fall out
I'd rather die.
I don't want to be here
To fry alive.
Don't protect me you megatron
I don't want to be here when a thousand

Suns lit up the sky
Don't protect me you neutron
I don't want to be here
To hear my children cry
Don't protect me you hydrogen
When ten million tons of rubble bury us alive
Don't protect me you moron
I don't want to see black rain falling from the sky.
I'd rather die.

TECHNOLOGY

I am a Machiavelli power lunatic
A computer, technological and video stereo freak
A million watts go thru me, amps and wire silicon.
Remote control and digital and quad and wireless phone
Bleeper bleep bleep and tweeter tweeter tweet my VHF's
    terrific
With some Schoenberg blasting through it

Technology/ that's food for me/
Steel and wire/I'm a space age sire
Laser beams/atomic waste/cobalt/
Radium you can taste/...technology!

My bike's a Harley Davidson, a thousand CC muscle/
A Ferrari for weekdays when I'm out at nights to hustle
I blast down the A40 hydraulic brakes on fire/
100 miles per hour and the slag screams out 'more
    power!'

Technology/ that's food for me
Remote control the missiles flow
Save the cities in a nuclear ray
That melts the brain but the buildings stay
Technology!

I smash down Oxford Street at night
Hear the whining siren
I leave a mass of broken legs
But they'll get bright new steel ones

Technology that's food for me
Steel and wire/I'm a space age sire/

227

Laser beams atomic waste
Cobalt/ radium you can taste technology!

My pacemaker's working perfectly
A steel cap rests inside my knee
A metal plate sits inside my brain
From overtaking on the inside lane
My soft lens fine
My kidney's tight
Climb in my lung machine at night

Technology that's food for me
Space age tarter/neon splat
Star wars is on the earth you prat
When the light comes
You will melt to fat/slow/
Technology

Lightning Source UK Ltd.
Milton Keynes UK
UKHW011542051220
374580UK00003B/62/J